Legacy of the Tetons

LEGACY OF THE TETONS

Homesteading in Jackson Hole

by

Candy Vyvey Moulton

tamarack books inc.

Book cover by Kathleen Petersen

Book design and typesetting by Typography by Gail Ward

ISBN 0-9634839-4-3

Cover photo by Abi Garaman is used with permission.
Copies of the photo are available from the
Ranch Shop, PO Box 1, Jackson Hole, Wy 83001.

Printed and bound in the United States of America

Published by Tamarack Books, Inc.
PO Box 190313
Boise, ID 83719-0313
1/800/962-6657

For Steve,
who first took me to Mormon Row
when I became his wife

Table of Contents

Acknowledgments

This book is the story of my children's forebears and those of many other children whom I've never met. It is a story of hard work and sacrifice with the goal of a better life in mind. Change the names and places and it could be about any of the thousands of people who immigrated to America or emigrated across the country to claim free land.

With any work of non-fiction, many people assist in its evolution. This project would never even have been started without the inspiration of the fine photographs of the historic Moulton Barn by Abi Garaman and the stories of Clark Moulton and Lester May.

Researching this story has been a delight. I've found tales for my children, Shawn and Erin Marie, they might otherwise never have known. In doing so, I neglected them at times, forgot to make cookies, and missed some of their school programs. I hope this final volume makes up for those lapses.

Many people assisted along the way. I particularly value the contributions of Larry Kummer, Dawn Ivison, and Rita Verley of the Teton County Historical Center, Ann Nelson of the Wyoming Department of Commerce Historical Research Division, Rick Ewig and the staff of the American Heritage Center at the University of Wyoming, Sharlene Milligan of the Grand Teton Natural History Association, Dubois artist Hannah Hinchman, Jackson photographer Olie Riniker, and Mabel James of Pinedale, who shared stories and photos.

I am particularly grateful to two women who traced this Mormon Row trail before I started my quest. Elizabeth Hayden researched and wrote about Jackson Hole many years ago, and her collection of notes, clippings, and other items became an invaluable aid to me. JoAnne Byrd interviewed some of the Mormon Row residents and the transcripts of her interviews, available at the Teton County Historical Center, gave me a wealth of first hand information from the people who lived on the Row. JoAnne also helped me locate necessary photos as the book came to its final phase of production.

I can never repay Clark and Veda Moulton for their love and sharing and providing me with a "home away from home" on Mormon Row whenever I needed a place to stay as I worked on this project for the past three years.

Lester and Melba May, Clark and Veda Moulton, Harley and Flossie Moulton, Helen Wise, Olie Riniker, and Penny Walters provided a valuable service by reading the manuscript. Thanks also to Win Blevins, Mike and Kathy Gear, and Shelly Ritthaler, who gave me so much advice and encouragement.

I am particularly indebted to my good friend and assistant editor at the Casper *Star-Tribune,* Dan Neal, who critiqued and commented on the manuscript when it was little more than a very rough draft. And I value the friendship and support of Kathy Gaudry, who, like me, believed this was a story that should be told.

Finally to Danny, Ila, Steve, Jerry, and David, this book is my lasting gift to you. May you cherish the stories.

—Candy Vyvey Moulton

Introduction

There are two places and two faces to Jackson Hole. The differences are both subtle and striking. First, there is Jackson Hole, a long valley completely surrounded by mountains and named for trapper David E. Jackson, a partner in the Rocky Mountain Fur Company. Then there is Jackson, the town at the south end of the hole.

To the thousands of people from throughout the world who visit Jackson every year it is western, but has trendy restaurants, resorts, and shopping. To the valley natives—there really are families who've lived in Jackson Hole for generations—it is a small town where the county fair is an important social event.

During the past one hundred years, Jacksonites have struggled with the elements and with development. Houses that sold for back taxes—just a few dollars—in the 1930s, turned over for $2,500 or $3,000 thirty years later and exchanged hands in another thirty years for between $150,000 and $200,000. The land in Grand Teton National Park that sold for thirty-nine dollars an acre to the Snake River Land Company in 1929, could have brought millions per acre by 1990.

Like all places, Jackson Hole and Jackson are more than land. They are home to a few thousand people who play host to a few hundred thousand every year.

Jackson has a different persona during the various seasons. In the springtime and the fall, its atmosphere is much like any other Wyoming community. Parking places are fairly easy to come by in front of downtown stores. There's seldom a line at the post office. The residents exchange friendly greetings because they actually know the people they meet on the street. During the winter, that same aura of hometown friendliness exists with a bit more traffic and fewer recognizable faces downtown.

During the summertime, however, Jackson undergoes a metamorphosis. From Memorial Day through Labor Day finding a downtown parking spot is next to impossible; just driving downtown is a trial as people fill the streets. The post office develops lines as do the restaurants, grocery stores, and other businesses. It's a bit as though the play *The Rat Race* comes to town for a three-month run. Through it all, Jackson prominently spots a cowboy image typified in downtown gunfights and cowboy music in bars where people can sit on a saddle as they bolt down a shot of whiskey.

Outside town, in Jackson Hole, *The Rat Race* has a limited summertime engagement as well. Traffic sometimes snarls on the Grand Teton National Park roads, but generally once you're away from the hubbub of town, the spirit of the place seeps into your soul and you find traveling forty-five miles per hour is not so bad after all. At that speed you see flowers and animals you'd miss at a faster pace.

Out in the Hole, you see a land in many ways like that seen

by the native Americans, the mountain men, and the home-steaders. Sagebrush and cottonwood trees form the backdrop for wild flowers: lupine, buttercups, and daisies. Elk, deer, moose, and buffalo still roam freely. Eagles and hawks catch the thermals. Although you will share the space with other people, a visit to Grand Teton National Park and Jackson Hole is a chance to experience the natural beauty of the land.

Park your vehicle and walk along the Gros Ventre or around Jenny Lake. Sit at dusk along the banks of the Snake and hear the birdsong. Position yourself on top of Signal Mountain in time for the sun to rise and watch the rays paint the land with color and hope and promise.

At the time the homesteaders drove their claim stakes on Mormon Row in 1896, few other people lived in this remote corner of Wyoming. No fences halted the movement of either wild or domestic animals. The Snake River raged every spring, spreading unchecked down its winding course.

That's what it was . . . . This is what it is.

The homesteaders tamed the land, cut and removed the native sage, built houses and barns. The government built a dam to harness the Snake, holding the water from a springtime rush and allowing its escape only in measured flows.

Now, for the most part, the homesteaders are just a memory to the land that is Grand Teton National Park. Most of their homes and barns are gone, or starting to rot. The sage is reclaiming its hold on the land. This country is not pristine, but much of it is natural in setting.

This is Jackson Hole . . . a land of the Indians, and the fur trappers; gathering spot for horse thieves and miners; domicile of homesteaders and home builders; habitat of buffalo and moose. There are sometimes wild and always wonderful stories about the people who've visited or called this place home.

Those stories are the legacy of the Tetons.

(Credit: Grand Teton Natural History Association)

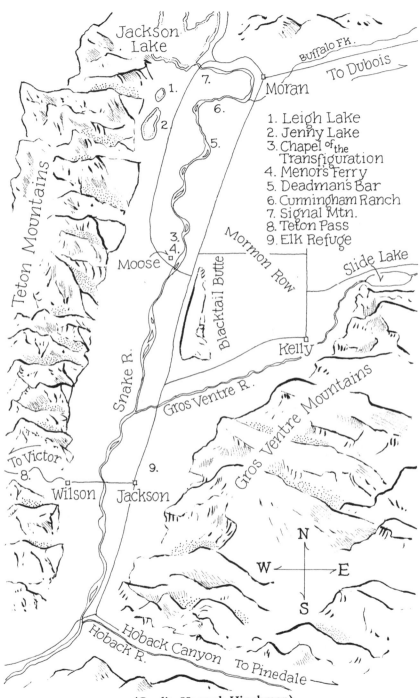

(Credit: Hannah Hinchman)

PART I

Feathers and Fur

Native Americans

When the deep winter snowpack melts from the mountain peaks at the headwaters of the Snake River, low-country grasses flourish. Natural lakes, all at the sources of the Snake River, are like jewels in the land. Generations ago as the first green spikes of springtime grass pushed their way toward the sun, elk, deer, and buffalo that wintered farther south along the Green River migrated over the mountain passes back to the hole.

Indians followed the wild game herds, which provided food and shelter—the keys to survival for people who lived off the bounty of the land. Mountains ring the valley of the Snake

River, tall jagged peaks on the west and less rugged, but still formidable ranges to the east and south. White men didn't know of the area when the various tribes made their annual pilgrimages to hunt the native wildlife. The area had abundant water and plenty of timber in the low lands to provide shelter during hot summer days.

Some Indians came from the Owl Creek Mountains to the east and up the North Fork of the Shoshone River to the large natural body of water that is now Yellowstone Lake. Others arrived by following the Wind River Valley nearly to its head-waters to reach the Gros Ventre fork of the Snake River, which they followed. Still more crossed into the hole over mountain passes now known as Togwotee, Union, Two Ocean, and Conant.

Three great families of Indians, the Algonquian, the Shoshoenean and the Siouan were in the area, represented by the Crow, Gros Ventre, Blackfeet, Nez Perce, Bannock, Eastern Shoshone, and Sheepeater tribes. Scattered all over the valley are traces of their campsites. Evidence of their occupation and passing is clear on Spread Creek, on Mosquito Creek, along the Gros Ventre, at Buck Mountain, and particularly along the shores of Jackson Lake.

The Crows spent most of their time in the valleys of the Yellowstone and Big Horn rivers, and they never claimed or occupied country beyond that area. However, they were wan-derers with an insatiable desire to steal horses. They roamed the West from the Black Hills to the Bitter Root Mountains and from the British lands to the Spanish provinces.

They found the wildlife-rich valley along the Snake River an ideal place to spend the summer because they could gather meat for long winters. The Bannocks and Shoshones, likewise, hunted the valley. The Atsinas, or Gros Ventres of the Prairies, habitually made a pilgrimage to visit their Arapaho relatives living on the South Platte. They went through Jackson Hole along the western base of the mountains that later would bear their name and into Green River country before trailing into what is now Colorado.

The Blackfeet were the most feared of the tribes in Jackson Hole. Perpetual fighters, the Blackfeet ranged in the country drained by the headwaters of the Missouri River generally in the area north of the Milk River in what is now northern Montana. But like the Crows, the Blackfeet made an annual pilgrimage to the broad Jackson valley to harvest and cure meat for wintertime use.

The Shoshonean family tribe homeland was around the southern, eastern, and western borders of the hole. One humble branch of that tribe, the Tukuarika or Sheepeaters, lived permanently in the area. Not fierce warriors or nomadic wanderers, the Sheepeaters, as their name implies, lived primarily off the mountain sheep.

The tribe, which may have been formed by Indian outcasts, had no horses and harvested the wild sheep for food and clothing by herding them into brush enclosures before killing them with bows and arrows. The Sheepeaters built the crude traps using some natural feature such as a steep cliff, bluff or rock outcropping.

Besides living off the bighorn sheep, the Indians also may have worshiped the animals. Bighorn skulls found embedded high in trees could be native shrines. Other tribes and the

Reclusive Sheepeater Indians are the only known year-around residents of the Jackson Hole and Yellowstone National Park areas prior to arrival of beaver trappers in the 1820s. (Photo Credit: Teton County Historical Center)

white men who later entered their territory scorned the Sheepeaters for they were considered hermits, seldom venturing away from their home grounds.

French trappers called them "les dignes de pitie" and referred to them as a "timid, harmless race" who lived in brush enclosures called wickiups. Chief Togwotee, who became the guide of the Shoshone Chief Washakie, is one famous member of the Sheepeaters and the natural pass over the mountains at the head of the Wind River bears the medicine man's name.

These tribes came to hunt game, to gather plentiful wild fruits and berries, and to fish. Early trappers found Indian trails on lines generally marked by today's highways.

The native Americans shared Jackson Hole with the mountain men during a thirty year period, but after the fur trade decline in the 1840s, had the place virtually to themselves for another thirty years before white men moved permanently to the valley in the late 1880s.

Looking
for Pelts

No known white man's feet crushed the native grasses or rippled the waters of the Snake River at the base of the jagged Teton mountain peaks before John Colter ventured into Jackson Hole in 1807. The six-foot-tall Virginian, a member of the Lewis and Clark expedition, was with the explorers in the fall of 1806 at the Mandan villages along the Missouri River when he met Illinois trappers and hunters Joseph Dickson and Forrest Hancock.

Those men were on their way toward the Yellowstone country. Lewis and Clark released Colter from his duties with their expedition so he could join Dickson and Hancock. As he turned westward again, Colter had a gun, ammunition, and supplies given to him by Lewis.

Following a winter of trapping with Dickson and Hancock, Colter started east, but he met Manuel Lisa who planned to establish a fur trading business in the Rocky Mountains. Upon persuasion by Lisa, Colter again faced westward. Lisa constructed a fort at the mouth of the Big Horn River andsent Colter to meet with the Crow Indians to barter for their furs.

During the winter of 1807, Colter began a journey into the area that was the source of the Snake River. Although some say Colter made a solitary trek, it's likely he had Crow Indian guides as he ventured up the Shoshone River, just west of present day Cody, to an area that was a steaming geyser basin and the original "Colter's Hell."

The mountain man's route is then clearly one of speculation. Some historians say he went up the Wind River to Union Pass and eventually down the Gros Ventre River, dropping into the broad hole—later called Jackson Hole—bounded by the Teton range to the west and the Gros Ventre and Wind River mountains to the south and east. Others claim he crossed into the valley over Togwotee Pass. Most agree, however, that Colter spent time near the foot of the Tetons. Why he did so is less crystalline.

Colter's goal was to locate the Indians and negotiate to buy furs, but he made the trek into the valley in winter—when no Indians lived there. His route isn't certain, but he made a loop around a water body he called Lake Biddle, which might have been Jackson Lake, before heading west to cross Teton Pass and see the area that later became known as Pierre's Hole and now is Idaho's Teton Basin.

Colter then probably headed east and north, perhaps crossing Conant Pass into a land where the ground was a bubbling cauldron of hot water and mud. Colter may have ventured south into Jackson Hole again before heading north to another water body he called "Lake Eustis," but which could be Yellowstone Lake. Colter's route is unclear—at least partially because the map he made with William Clark in 1814 is so inaccurate. It doesn't clearly define the Snake River, but few dispute the claim that he was in Jackson Hole in 1807, at a time when the last settled outpost was hundreds of miles away in St. Louis.

During the next three years Colter trapped, explored, and on at least one occasion engaged in a race for his life against Blackfeet Indians. Then in 1810, Colter returned to St. Louis where he outlined his travels during the previous years to his former commander, William Clark. He helped prepare the first map of the region that is now northwest Wyoming.

That winter of 1810–11 John Hoback, Edward Robinson, and Jacob Reznor made the second known visit to the area by white men. They entered the hole from the west by crossing Teton Pass and likely trapped and hunted before leaving the area traveling over Togwotee Pass. The three headed to Missouri, but fell short of their goal when they met the Astorians on their westward journey in the fall of 1811. Organized by John Jacob Astor in 1810, the American Pacific Fur Company's Astorians wanted to wrest the western fur trade from the British Hudson's Bay and French Canadian Northwest fur companies.

The Astorians sent two parties to the northwest that year, one by sea and the other by land. The overland Astorians were the first significant transcontinental expedition since Lewis and Clark blazed their route. The leader was Wilson Price Hunt of New Jersey, a man ill-equipped to handle the rigors of frontier life. It was their good fortune that they met Hoback, Robinson, and Reznor, who agreed to return to the West as guides. The party crossed the plains to the Big Horn Mountains and the Wind River, which they followed.

The guides and friendly Indians assured Hunt if he followed the Wind he would only need to traverse one mountain pass to drop into the headwaters of the Columbia River, but scarce game left Hunt reluctant to take the advice. When the party crossed a beaten Indian trail that headed west, Hunt veered from the Wind. Therefore, instead of following the Wind River to its source and crossing the mountains at Togwotee Pass, Hunt went south and west.

From one vantage point the party could see the needle-sharp peaks of the mountains that formed the backdrop for the Snake River. The guides said the mountains were at the source of the Snake and they called the peaks Pilot Knobs, which became the first official name for the distinctive range.

The party eventually hit the Hoback River and followed it into Jackson Hole. When Hunt and the Astorians left the hole to resume their journey, four men remained. During the winter of 1811-12 the four, American Alexander Carson, and French Canadians Louis St. Michel, Pierre Detayé, and Pierre Delaunay, trapped the beaver-rich streams. By springtime luxurious pelts filled packs on their horses as they crossed Teton Pass headed west to the fort Hunt planned at the Columbia River mouth.

Their journey took a grim twist not long after the four left the hole when Crows attacked, killing Detayé and robbing the others of their beaver pelts. They lost the winter's effort in a quick raid.

From its discovery by Colter in 1807 until those first trappers lived in the area in the winter of 1811, the Teton valley remained pristine; an area for the Indians to hunt and fish during the summers, but of little use in wintertime. Before that snowy season of solitary trapping in 1811–12, no white men had lived in the hole and likely only the reclusive Sheepeater Indians had seen many of the harsh winter days at the source of the Snake.

In the fall of 1812, seven Astorian trappers returning from Oregon Country lost their horses in a stampede caused by Indians in present-day central Idaho. The Astorians built a raft and ascended the Snake for more than a hundred miles before crossing into Pierre's Hole and spotting the familiar Pilot Knobs. They eventually crossed into Jackson Hole and journeyed up the Hoback River to the plains. There they wandered aimlessly before finding a break in the mountains—South Pass—that became the key to western migration.

Except for the trip through Jackson Hole their route was much the same as the Oregon Trail pathway. Because they were the first white men to locate South Pass, those Astorians often get credit for discovery of the Oregon Trail route, although Indians used it for generations.

The War of 1812 brought the fur trade to a virtual standstill. Few people visited the area marked by the rugged mountains until 1819 when Donald McKenzie of the Northwest

Company explored there. He noted that the most remarkable heights in America's backbone were the three mountains designated as the Pilot Knobs. It was during that era, however, that the jagged peaks got another name. French trappers called them "les trois tetons" or "The Three Breasts."

Jedediah Smith, Jim Bridger, William Sublette, and David E. Jackson in 1822 joined William H. Ashley and Major Andrew Henry when they advertised for "one hundred young men to ascend the Missouri River to its source" on a trapping expedition for the Rocky Mountain Fur Company. Although most joining the party were still in their teens, many made a lasting mark on the history of the West as they pioneered routes to California, Utah, and Montana and left their names on mountains, valleys, and streams.

After leaving St. Louis, Henry headed up the Missouri River for the mouth of the Yellowstone. Along the Missouri the trappers engaged in a bitter battle with Arikara Indians that caused them to turn back. It was fall of 1823 before they went by horse and mule to the Shining Mountains, better known as the Rockies. The following spring hostile Blackfeet confronted and killed many trappers who encroached onto their territory.

Henry refused to give up. He divided the men into smaller expeditions, and sent them to search for prime hunting and trapping grounds. Thomas Fitzpatrick crossed the natural break in the mountains eventually called South Pass, as he headed toward the Green River in 1824, earning credit for relocating the western gateway. Meanwhile, Jedediah Smith took a party of seven trappers into the Teton area. Few had been in the hole since Colter and the Astorians passed through more than a decade earlier, so Smith gets distinction for rediscovering the area. Smith entered by following the Hoback River and left by crossing Conant Pass.

That fall Ashley inaugurated the tradition known as *rendezvous* when he gathered trappers under Andrew Henry and Jedediah Smith on Black's Fork of the Green River. The era of the fur trade was in full swing, with demand high for the beaver pelts that grew luxurious in the cold mountain streams of the West.

By fall of 1825 Jim Bridger and Thomas Fitzpatrick, accompanied by thirty trappers, followed Smith's route into Jackson Hole. With their venture the Teton valley became a center of trapping operations, but it wasn't until 1829 that the area received its present-day name.

A Name for
the Area

David E. Jackson, one man in Ashley and Henry's original party, was in the mountains continuously after 1823. In his thirties, he was considerably older than most in the company and it is likely that he worked in a clerical capacity rather than as an expedition leader. He was a steadying influence among the more boisterous younger men.

Jackson was on the Bear River in 1826 right after the summer rendezvous in Utah's Cache Valley when he joined William Sublette and Jedediah Smith in purchasing the Rocky Mountain Fur Company from Ashley. Smith became the explorer, Jackson the field manager, and Sublette made the annual trek back to Missouri to sell furs. Jackson spent his time in the mountains, directing the activities of the company trappers, and Snake River country was his favorite haunt. In 1827 the company had about half a million dollars worth of furs for Sublette to take down the Missouri. Before he left, the partners agreed to meet at the head of the Snake in 1829.

Jackson kept no diaries of his journeys during the next two years, but he likely spent at least part of the time near the Teton range. He lived there the winter of 1828–29 and in the summer of 1829 William Sublette, who led his company up the Wind River and across Togwotee Pass, joined him. The two partners met at the lake that now carries Jackson's name. After their meeting, Jackson and Sublette pushed westward over Teton Pass searching for Smith whom they eventually located in Pierre's Hole.

Although local legend is that Jackson's Hole and Jackson's Lake received names during that summer of 1829, it is likely the locale went by his name even earlier since it was a favorite trapping spot of Jackson. Thus the name may have been gradually acquired rather than suddenly bestowed. Over the years the possessive has been dropped in both cases.

In 1829 Jackson, Smith, and Sublette sold their firm to the Rocky Mountain Fur Company. Jackson left the mountains in 1830 and headed for Santa Fe and California before eventually returning to St. Louis in 1832. What became of him after that is somewhat of a mystery. Some believe he took off with property belonging to three other men and others claim he spent the large and hard-earned fortune he had made in the fur trade in a short period of years. He died on Christmas Eve, 1837.

Trappers traded their furs and obtained supplies at locations all around Jackson Hole, but the area itself never hosted a major gathering.

Comparative quiet settled on Jackson Hole for nearly forty-five years. A few prospectors looking for gold checked out the area in the 1860s and 1870s. In 1872 the Hayden survey of Yellowstone country named many geographical features including Mount Moran, Mount St. John, Leigh, Jenny, Taggert and Bradley lakes, and Mount Leidy.

Artist Thomas Moran visited the area in 1879. On August 23 he wrote in his diary:

The Tetons are now plainly visible but not well defined owing to mistiness of the atmosphere. They loom grandly above all the other mountains, an intervening ridge dividing us from the Teton Basin stretches for miles to the north of a beautiful pinkish yellow with delicate shades of pale cobalt while the distant range is of an exquisite blue with but little definition of forms on their surfaces.

Forest fires of unknown origin charred the area that summer as Moran made his visit to a land previously seen only by Indians, trappers, and government explorers. The time was not far away when the first settlers would venture over the high mountain passes to the spectacular Jackson Hole.

PART II

A Place to Call Home

The First
Homesteaders

The first permanent settlers in Jackson Hole moved in from the south. John Holland and his friend, Johnny Carnes, built cabins on the Little Gros Ventre River, a stream known today as Flat Creek, that meanders through the National Elk Refuge.

Born in Steubenville, Ohio, Johnny Carnes fought for the Union during the Civil War, but shortly after its final battle he headed west to settle on Fontenelle Creek near LaBarge, in southwest Wyoming. For a time Carnes carried the LaBarge mail. Then on March 17, 1881, he married Millie, a half Ute, half German woman. She had no children, but they adopted an Indian boy, Charles Harmes.

Johnny Carnes and his wife Millie, were among the first to live year around in Jackson Hole. Here Carnes, center, is shown with his brother and another man. (Photo Credit: Teton County Historical Center)

Holland spent his time trapping and timbering near LaBarge and Cokeville. He became familiar with Jackson Hole by chasing beaver there in the 1870s. In the summer of 1883,

John Holland was one of the first homesteaders in Jackson Hole, settling permanently in 1884. (Photo Credit: Teton County Historical Center)

Holland, Carnes, Millie, and probably Charles, went up the Green River, crossed Bacon Ridge, and then followed the Gros Ventre to Jackson Hole. That is the route many early-day travelers to Jackson Hole used, but ironically is not a main highway into the valley today.

Upon arrival the venturers built a cabin for the Carnes family. It's unclear whether they spent the winter in Jackson Hole or if they headed south with the elk to Green River country, but in 1884 the four were back in Jackson Hole building a cabin for Holland. From then on for the next decade they spent most of their time in the isolated Jackson Hole valley. Holland and Carnes filed on the first water rights in Jackson Hole and hand-dug irrigation ditches for their hay ground.

Jackson Hole soon became a home to many bachelors— who likely were mainly a bunch of horse thieves and others on the dodge. Carnes and Holland played constant hosts to the surge of single men in the valley. Holland often went on horseback or on snowshoes over Teton Pass to Victor, Idaho, to get the mail. On one such trip he met Maude Carpenter, whom he married in the 1890s. Not long after their wedding, they sold the homestead to D. H. Goe and moved to Scio, Oregon.

Johnny and Millie Carnes got the patent to their homestead in 1897, but they were no longer living full time in Jackson Hole. In 1895 the Carneses moved to the Fort Hall Reservation in Idaho to live on an eighty acre tract Millie owned. Goe also bought their homestead. Both the Carnes and Holland homesteads are now a part of the National Elk Refuge lands, just north of Jackson.

The first all white family came to Jackson Hole in 1888 when Martin Nelson, his wife and four-year-old daughter, Cora, arrived. Mrs. Nelson tied her flatirons on one side of the saddle and her coffee pot on the other as she and Cora rode a saddle horse over the pass. Nelson homesteaded in the swampy part of Flat Creek and for his effort earned the never-to-be-forgotten nickname, "Slough Grass" Nelson.

First
Wagons Enter
the Hole

Indians first used most historic routes leading into Jackson Hole and the beaver trappers followed them. The Teton Pass crossing from Victor, Idaho, became identified as Hunt's Pass, for Wilson Price Hunt who crossed it in 1811. In 1886 Joe Infanger and Adolph Miller drove the first wagons over Teton Pass where they claimed the fifth and sixth homesteads in the valley that still had mostly bachelors as residents.

All that started to change in 1889 when Mormon bishop Sylvester Wilson of Wilsonville, Utah, joined by his son-in-law Selar Cheney, and his oldest son, Ervin and their wives, left

The road over Teton Pass was just a steep single track when the first settlers moved into Jackson Hole and it didn't see much improvement for many years. (Photo Credit: Teton County Historical Center)

Utah in search of a better place to raise their stock and their families.

The Wilsons first stopped in Salem, Idaho. There they learned Sylvester's brother Nick was in Jackson Hole harvesting hay. The Wilsons' covered wagons headed north to St. Anthony, Idaho, where the men cut logs for a house. They had it partially built when Nick Wilson returned from Jackson with stories of a grand valley and plenty of hay to feed cattle during the winter.

The families chewed on the idea of sending the young men to the valley with the cattle, but then decided the entire party would move to Jackson Hole for the winter. Some went ahead to harvest feed and in crossing over the pass, they had to take the wagon apart and move two wheels at a time. They also widened the trail by cutting trees.

Upon arriving in Jackson Hole they borrowed a mowing machine owned by one area bachelor and put up their hay on Slough Grass Nelson's ranch. It was November 1889 before the rest of the family made the trek over the pass. They stocked six covered wagons with flour and grain in Rexburg and Wilford, Idaho, but later cached much of the supply on the west side of Teton Pass.

It took two weeks to move across Teton Pass from St. Anthony. In making the trip, the Wilsons chopped more trees to further widen the road and took one large wheel from the back of the wagon putting both big wheels on the downhill side for better load balance on the steep terrain. Six-horse hitches pulled each wagon to the summit. On the downhill trip, men roughlocked the wheels and dragged trees to slow the speed of the wagon. For many years both grades to the summit had to be descended only with the aid of roughlocks—large untrimmed trees chained to the wheels to prevent their turning.

When the families got to Jackson, November 11, 1889, it was too late to build cabins, so those already living in the valley opened their doors. John Carnes, who had just built a new cabin, gave the use of his old one to the Sylvester Wilsons. Will Crawford shared his cabin with the Nick Wilsons, John Holland took in the Selar Cheneys, and John Cherry opened his home to the Ervin Wilsons.

The 1889 Jackson Hole Christmas celebration took place at the home of Will Crawford with a menu featuring elk steaks, wild geese and ducks, vegetables, plum pudding, mince pies, and doughnuts fried in bear grease. The day was filled with music, dancing, and a midnight supper.

It was a rough first winter in Jackson Hole, according to an account by Ervin's wife, Mary Jane, who was eighteen and the mother of a six-week-old son. Both of the Wilsons' milk cows died and she brought her baby through that season of short days on elk soup. The grown-ups lived on elk meat and water gravy. Loneliness engulfed Mary Jane as mail arrived only twice from November until May. Men who were good on snowshoes made the hazardous trek over Teton Pass for letters. Bachelor Hy Adams got a newspaper with a serial story that he loaned to everyone, passing it among families until it was in tatters.

Finally Easter arrived and the settlers gathered at John Holland's where they sang hymns, heard a moving sermon by Sylvester Wilson, and thanked God for guiding them to the beautiful valley.

As warmer temperatures started melting the snowpack and wildflowers poked their noses toward the sun, Sylvester rode through Jackson Hole and saw that the snow thawed first in an area the bachelors called Big Flat, today known as South Park. He decided that was where his descendents would settle. Each Wilson family built a two room cabin with a fireplace in one end and cookstove in the other room. The log cabins had small poles placed closely together and covered with dirt to form a roof.

Sylvester Wilson soon cleared the sagebrush from ten acres of land. Mary Wilson had enough Barred Rock chickens to start a flock for everyone and the families were self sufficient. The women made buckskin gloves, moccasins, and buckskin suits for the men, often obtaining the buckskin from Indian women who camped near their land. Men loaded cartridges and poured their bullets in a mold. They made bedsteads from poles with strips of raw elk hide woven from side to side to serve as springs, and topped with a ticking mattress filled with hay, and sometimes a feather mattress on top of that.

The wives had dishes of heavy china, knives and forks of steel with wooden handles, and cooking pots mostly of iron. Mary Wilson had a large brass kettle she used for making soap and heating wash water. To soften the water, the women put it in a barrel half full of wood ashes.

Everyday dresses were of calico and gingham, but the women made their "best" Sunday dresses of alpaca, cashmere, linsey, and brilliantine, with long sleeves and skirts that nearly touched the floor. Some wore basques and bustles and most had two petticoats to make the dress stand out properly. They curled their hair on a heated spike or with paper or rags.

Wilson

The small town of Wilson takes its name from the first family to bring numerous wagons over Teton Pass. Elijah "Uncle Nick" Wilson is one of those truly colorful western heroes who had a real life far more exciting than most. He spent two childhood years among the Shoshone Indians as the adopted son of the mother of the great chief Washakie and was the hero of H.R. Driggs' *The White Indian Boy or Uncle Nick Among the Shoshones*. He not only lived with the Shoshonis, but he also rode for the short-lived Pony Express, served in the army, and drove stagecoaches before helping his family settle in Jackson Hole.

In 1893 Ed Blair homesteaded on the east bank of the Snake River, and started the second ferry service in the valley; the first was upstream at Moose. Uncle Nick started the town of Wilson near the ferry in 1895.

More development came to Wilson in 1896 when Warren and Lucy Edmiston arrived and he opened a blacksmith shop. He'd learned the trade from his father and grandfather. Warren soon had the nickname "Pap" and he offered services of all kinds, including pulling teeth to save people the trip of crossing Teton Pass and going to St. Anthony, Idaho, to a real dentist.

Wilson got its first post office in 1898, managed by Matilda Wilson, Nick's wife. She died a year later so Nick became postmaster for three years and also operated the town's hotel and first general store, which once was characterized in the Gasoline Alley comic strip. When the Gros Ventre Slide occurred in 1925, Wilson townsite saw no impact, but the Kelly Flood two years later affected the small community when rising waters spread six feet deep, damaging land and buildings and killing hundreds of cattle.

Marysvale First, then Jackson

Other families followed the Wilsons and a town started at the site of the post office, just north of present day Jackson. The embryo town went by the name Marysvale, named after Mary White, the first postmistress. Robert Miller's wife, Grace, purchased land from John Simpson just south of Marysvale and her husband, a banker, real estate developer, and first supervisor of the Jackson Hole Forest Preserve, laid out a new town in 1897 just to the south of Marysvale. It had few buildings by 1900 and officially incorporated as Jackson in 1901. Grace Miller not only located the townsite, she later had another role in its history.

Jackson residents pause for a photo. From left: Lew Fleming, Virgil Ward, Ercel Ward, Charlie McConnell, Pete Linn and unidentified man. (Photo Credit: Teton County Historical Center)

By 1909 Jackson had about two hundred people, while the Jackson Hole population neared fifteen hundred, according to the first issue of the *Jackson's Hole Courier*, January 28, 1909. There were nine post offices in the valley located at Jackson, Cheney, Elk, Moran, Grovont, Zenith, Brooks, Wilson, and Teton. Six-day-a-week mail service came from St. Anthony, Idaho, to Wilson and Jackson.

The schools were "at least up to standard" and Jackson Hole boasted three sawmills on the west side of the valley. It's said the first of those mills used trees that settlers dragged to the bottom of Teton Pass as roughlocks on wagons and the supply was sufficient to keep the mill in operation for a couple of years.

In Jackson, businesses included two general stores, a drug store, hotel, restaurant, feed and livery barn, blacksmith shop, and saloon. The community had a schoolhouse, a Mormon church, and a club house. The Episcopal Mission announced plans it would build a church during the summer. That log structure, St. John's Church, still serves its congregation, and is the site of many community functions, including the filming of church scenes in the movie classic *Spencer's Mountain*.

Jackson quickly became the largest town in the Hole. Farther north, communities formed around the sections claimed by homesteaders.

Just getting to Jackson Hole was a chore, particularly during the deep snows of winter time. In this scene some men are hauling gas over Teton Pass. (Photo Credit: Teton County Historical Center)

PART III

Mormon Row

A Symbol for America

Often tourists ask, "How long have you lived here?" We'll answer "Quite awhile, our grandparents homesteaded. The Tetons were just little fellows when we come in. We watched 'em grow up!"

— Clark Moulton

Heavy wet snow causes the leafed-out branches on the cottonwood trees along a single-lane dirt road in Grand Teton National Park to droop as if in meditation. As the sun rises over the Gros Ventre Range, it illuminates the peaks of the Tetons and then the sagebrush and grass range that is Antelope Flats. The rays of the May sun turn the snow to slush and mud along the road.

The moisture and the sun's rays illuminate the weathered wood on a pitched-roofed barn that is inspiration to artists and painters. The Moulton Barn was a homestead's necessity. It, like the land, was to be the heritage for a family, but both have

35

become the domain of an entire nation. They are a poor man's legacy.

U

Thomas Alma Moulton could barely scrape together the money for nails when he built the first section of his barn, a barn that was the key element of his Jackson Hole homestead. The lush western Wyoming grassland at the foot of the Tetons enticed Alma, the name he went by, to pull up his Idaho roots, where he had first settled his family and to replant them in northwest Wyoming.

T.A. Moulton's barn, 1974. (Photo Credit: Olie Riniker)

Alma was one of about a dozen Mormon emigrants who staked land in the area that became known as Mormon Row. It was not an easy move and it was not an easy life, but the land was free, the soil rich, and the area uncrowded. They chose their homesteads based on quality of the soil. They gave little consideration to the fact that their homes were at the altar of the Tetons. It was a community of determined, hardworking men and women who built a school for the education of their children and a church for the worship of their God.

U

Long before the homesteaders came, when the buds burst on the trees and new shoots of grass poked through the melting snow, the first people known to venture into the valley of the Snake River crossed the mountain passes. They were the native Americans. The long, lush valley abounded with game and wild fruits. It was a perfect place for the various tribes to summer.

The Indians harvested the abundant food supply and trapped along the clear streams. When the deep snows of winter came, they trekked back over the mountains, the Wind Rivers, the Gros Ventres, or the Tetons to spend cold, snowy days and nights in their villages far from the harsh, isolated valley.

That way of life changed for the native Americans in 1807 when John Colter's white feet crossed the verdant valley. He had come in search of the Indians to barter with them for their furs for the trading companies.

In the lingo of the mountain man, a valley ringed by mountains was called a hole and other trappers followed Colter to the one he had found. Frenchmen and Englishmen and Americans sought beaver in the free flowing streams. The fur trade was in decline by the late 1830s and nearly petered out by the early 1840s.

Comparative quiet settled on Jackson Hole for nearly forty-five years; the beaver built their dams and swam in their ponds endangered only by the Indians and a limited number of trappers. A few prospectors looked for gold, but there were no big strikes like Sutter's Mill in California or the Yukon to attract hoards of miners.

∪

It wasn't until the 1880s that anyone settled permanently. The first were two men named John, one Indian woman, and her adopted son. Then bachelors, who built dugouts or cabins, planted gardens, started raising cattle, and may have rustled horses, claimed land. Only those few bachelors and a small number of families lived in Jackson Hole when James I. May rode through the area in 1894 in search of fertile ground.

The Idaho man sought a place to grow crops and raise his

children when he ventured around Blacktail Butte one spring day. There the sagebrush was belly-deep to his horse, the land was level, and the Gros Ventre River traversed the eastern portion of the flat. He knew tall sagebrush meant rich, fertile soil.

James chose a section of the land he liked and determined that he would settle in Jackson Hole. He mounted his horse and returned to Idaho for his family. It took two years to organize his goods, gather horses and cattle, and save the money he needed for a homesteading venture in Wyoming.

May waited for the snow to clear from high mountain passes and in July 1896, he returned to Jackson Hole accompanied by other Idahoans in search of a place to call home. Though many homesteaders who claimed land near May shared family relationships and a religion, not all were relatives or members of the same church.

Those men intended to live their lives along the lane that became Mormon Row. They planned to pass their knowledge and their land on to their children and grandchildren. Such an

Clark and Veda Moulton on an evening walk down Mormon Row, where they have lived all their lives. (Photo Credit: Jackson Hole *News*/Bill Willcox)

inheritance might have been fulfilled except that wealthy phil-
anthropist John D. Rockefeller visited the area. He saw the
beauty and the promise of the land. A company, unobtrusively
backed by Rockefeller, formed to purchase the land that—after
years of wrangling—Congress set aside as Grand Teton
National Park.

∪

Clark Moulton, eldest son of Alma Moulton, and Veda May
Moulton, granddaughter of James I. May, have lived all their
lives on Mormon Row. Her birth took place at one end of the
lane and he came as an infant to the other. They met at the
church and schoolhouse halfway between each of their childhood homes and have lived together for more than fifty years
on land that was part of the Moulton homestead. In 1994 they
owned the only privately-held acre along Mormon Row.

Every morning they sit down to breakfast at their dining
room table, give thanks to God for their bounty, and watch the
weather patterns over the Teton range. Whether the peaks are
lit in sunshine, shrouded in fog, or glistening with snow, they
never tire of the sight. Together they recall the dreams of their
homesteading forefathers and tell stories to preserve their
heritage.

Pushing West
for Free Land

Frequently I have observed wagons pass by my house with one starving yoke of cattle to drag them and the family straggling on foot behind.
— Mountain Man James Beckwourth

Starting in 1843, Wyoming saw a plethora of visitors—emigrants seeking a better life and greater opportunity in Oregon and Washington, riches in the gold fields of California and Montana, or religious freedom in Utah.

They came along the Oregon Trail following the North Platte River to Fort Laramie and Deer Creek. Those adventurers carved their names in the rock at Register Cliff and crossed the muddy river near what would eventually be Fort Caspar. Their journey took them to Independence Rock, past Devil's Gate and Split Rock, and up the Sweetwater River to South Pass.

Oregon Trail ruts deepened under the wagon wheels of families spurred to cross the continent in search of land. The prolonged depression that swept the country in 1837 combined with the adventurous spirit of some people. That and the opportunity to explore new regions gave emigrants the impetus to pack belongings and cross the prairie.

Some 350,000 emigrants traveled the Oregon-California-Mormon trail corridor from 1843 to 1873. The key to the migration was South Pass as shown. (Photo Credit: Wyoming State Museum)

By 1839 Oregon Societies had formed in Mississippi valley towns and the emigration was in full swing by 1843 when the first large wagon train, involving about one thousand people headed west. Entire families heaped their baggage, hitched their teams, and started for Oregon. Before long the trail became a road upon which thousands of Americans traveled. Though they had canvas-covered wagons for their belongings, few rode. Most walked. They set out in anticipation of a better life ahead and if their steps were light at first, the emigrants soon found the trail that paralleled the Platte, Sweetwater, and Snake rivers was one of drudgery and tragedy.

Mountain man Jim Beckwourth, well-known as a tall-tale teller, in one instance probably accurately portrayed the plight of the emigrants: "Frequently I have observed wagons pass by my house with one starving yoke of cattle to drag them and the family straggling on foot behind."

From 1843 until 1862 some 350,000 men, women and children, followed the Oregon Trail. Difficulties laced the path as they forded the rivers and streams, and suffered from blistering heat and biting cold. They littered the trail with their possessions as they reduced loads on heavily-laden wagons to make traveling easier for trail-worn stock.

In shallow graves sometimes marked with stones or a crude cross, they buried loved ones—those who started the trip in anticipation, but who failed to finish the journey. They died of injury and illness. Cholera and accidents took their toll.

On the plains of Nebraska the pioneers collected buffalo chips for fuel, but after they crossed the Continental Divide at South Pass they were in Oregon Country where there were few buffalo. In areas where trees were scarce, overlanders burned sagebrush and remains of wagons found broken and abandoned by the trail. They appreciated the sacrifice of those who had traveled the road before. The landscape was forbidding as Amelia Stewart Knight wrote in her diary on June 11, 1853:

> We crossed this afternoon over the roughest and most desolate piece of ground that was ever made. . . . Not a drop of water, nor a spear of grass to be seen, nothing but barren hills, bare and broken rock, sand and dust.

The Oregon and California Trail pioneers flowed across the land in spite of the obstacles—disease, dangerous river crossings, accidents, and occasionally hostile Indians—until they reached their destination, which might have been Oregon, but was more likely California. Few of the early travelers remained in what is now Wyoming. They crossed the land, followed its rivers, saw its mountains and deserts, but kept on moving.

The Oregon Trail paralleled the Mormon Trail that followed the north bank of the Platte River across Indian territory that would become Nebraska and Wyoming. Unlike the pioneers of the Oregon-California route who sought land or gold, the Mormons, led by Brigham Young, wanted safety from the religious persecution they had endured in Missouri and Illinois.

When Brigham Young started his flock's western migration he had no destination in mind. He said only that the Latter-day Saints were going to a place over the mountains that would be a new home. They headed for Zion.

Before venturing to the Great Salt Lake Valley, the Mormons saw many of their leaders killed or falsely imprisoned. Heading west they kept to the north bank of the North Platte River. They didn't want to run the risk of further conflict with the people traveling along the southern bank. Also, the first wave of Mormon emigrants established permanent camps where those who followed could stop. The early travelers planted crops to be harvested by Mormons passing later in the seasons.

Among those who followed the Mormon Trail during its early days was the family of James L. May. He was just twenty in 1852 when his parents, George and Hannah May, left England for Utah. Their ocean voyage was harsh with headwinds and bad weather. Before they arrived at the mouth of the Mississippi River they were out of water and had only rice and musty oatmeal to eat.

James and George headed overland for Council Bluffs, Iowa. A week later they grieved when a messenger told them the boat carrying their family exploded, killing all on board. Fortunately, the story was not accurate. Hannah and the other six children were safe and uninjured except for seventeen-year-old Harriet who hurt her left foot. Other families weren't so lucky as the fire destroyed the boat. About thirty people drowned or received burns.

Finally in mid-June of 1852, the May family reunited in Council Bluffs. Tragedy soon reared its ugly head as first George and two daughters—Elizabeth, the eldest at age twenty-two, and Emily, the youngest at age nine—died of cholera. Hannah and her remaining children started for the ferry on the Missouri River to begin their trek on the Mormon Trail. Before they left, eleven-year-old Wilam died. In a final blow on July 2, 1852, Hannah died of consumption. She went to her shallow, dirt grave without a coffin.

Four children survived, ranging in age from thirteen to twenty. Those orphans set out on the 1,036 mile, nearly four-month-long trek from Iowa to Utah. They arrived at Salt Lake on October 14, 1852.

Besides the Mormon and Oregon Trails, other routes across Wyoming developed including the Bozeman, Bridger, Cherokee, and Overland pathways. In 1867 and 1868 the Union Pacific Railroad pushed across Wyoming. The coming of the railroad brought increasing numbers of settlers, particularly those who wanted to claim free land in the West made available by the Homestead Act of 1862.

For many in later years that legislation was a chance to begin a new life far from the Civil War-torn south. For others it was an opportunity to own land. A homestead could be claimed by any man twenty-one years old or the head of a family, who was a United States' citizen or in the process to become one, and who had never fought against the United States.

The land up for grabs was the hundreds of thousands of unappropriated public acres primarily west of the Mississippi River. In order to gain title, the claimant had to live on it for at least six months every year for a five year period, and make improvements, including a twelve by twelve cabin.

After five years of development, the land became the homesteader's property. For those not wanting to wait so long, title also could be obtained by paying $1.25 per acre under a process known as *pre-emption*. The government hoped to keep the land out of the hands of developers, but wasn't entirely successful as people often worked their way around the law. Some built their cabins on wheels to move from one tract to another.

Propaganda about the good life available on free land in the West combined with a shortage of land elsewhere and resulted in a swarm of pioneers claiming homestead tracts. During the period from 1862 until 1890 settlers brought more new U.S. soil under cultivation than in the previous two and a half centuries.

Congress wanted land in the hands of individuals with small, independent farms when it limited the size of a homestead claim to 160 acres. The nation's leaders failed to recognize—or chose to ignore—the fact that most of the prairie opened to homesteading wouldn't begin to support a family on a farm that size.

As the development of western trails shows, settlers headed for the fertile valleys of Oregon, Utah, and California. Most passed across the great expanse of land that in 1868 became Wyoming Territory.

An amendment to the Homestead Act in 1872 allowed Civil War veterans to deduct their months of service from the five year residency requirement. A necessary fee ranged from eighteen to thirty-four dollars.

The 1873 Timber Culture Act entitled a person to 160 acres. To "prove up" on the land, the homesteader had to plant and keep growing forty acres of trees for eight years. That obligation was reduced to ten acres of trees in 1878. While many people eventually got title to their land under the Homestead Act of 1862, only about ten percent of those who tried were successful under the Timber Culture Act. In Wyoming, of the 3,123 Timber Culture Act filings, just 333 led to final entry under the law.

The Desert Act of 1877 allowed purchase or claim of up to 640 acres of desert land, which needed irrigation water before cultivation was possible. For twenty-five cents an acre settlers could occupy the land for three years, then for an additional dollar an acre they could obtain title. Many paid the twenty-five cent fee and used the desert land to graze their cattle or sheep, never intending to make the irrigation improvements necessary to own the land.

In the 1870s and 1880s, the population of Wyoming Territory started to grow. It was a period when tides of immigrants from foreign lands swept across the ocean. Settlers moved into the Big Horn Basin and the upper North Platte River Valley, but Jackson Hole remained pristine.

It wasn't until 1884 that the first men tramped over the forbidding mountains to claim land in Jackson Hole. Early ranchers on Mormon Row—starting in 1896—filed claims using the various provisions of homestead law. Jackson Hole was no longer a forgotten area of Wyoming as the settlers poured over the passes to make their claims.

West with a
Handcart

*Every death weakened our forces. In my hundred I could not raise enough men
to pitch a tent when we camped.*

—Willie Company member John Chislett

The labor pains started two days out into the Irish Channel off the shore of England. As the *Thornton* rocked and pitched on the ocean waves, Sarah Moulton gave birth to Charles Alma Moulton, her seventh child, on May 6, 1856. Charles was so tiny and frail that his family carried him on a pillow from his birth until his family reached Salt Lake City, Utah, six months later.

That he survived the journey over the Atlantic to New York, and then across part of America with an ill-fated company of Mormon immigrants pushing and pulling handcarts to join Brigham Young in Utah, is a miracle to some. It certainly was to his family, but they expected the triumph since the family firmly believed in the blessing Sarah received before leaving England. Mormon missionaries promised her if the family followed its faith to America, the parents and children would survive the journey.

U

Sarah surprised her husband, Thomas, by secretly stashing money in a fruit jar for fifteen years until she had enough to pay costs for a move to America. The family included Thomas' eldest daughter, Sarah, nineteen, and the children of Thomas and his second wife, also named Sarah. They were Mary Ann (fifteen), William (thirteen), Joseph (eleven), James Heber (eight), Charlotte (five), and Sophia Elizabeth (three).

The pilgrimage was perilous even before it began. Just before the departure date, the children had smallpox. Though they all recovered, one girl still had a pox mark on her left wrist as the family prepared to board the ship. Wearing a glove on her left hand, the family earnestly prayed while an official made an inspection. Their prayers were answered. The pox-marked hand was never revealed.

Aboard the *Thornton* with 764 immigrants of Danish, Swedish, and English nationality, the Moultons subsisted on rice, sugar, and musty oats. They suffered through the terror of a fire on the ship before reaching the still waters of New York Harbor on June 14, 1856.

Their mode of transportation then shifted to the railroad for the journey to Iowa City, Iowa, where the Mormon handcart companies organized. There the Moultons had to wait for construction of 250 handcarts built mostly of green, unseasoned timber. Each handcart carried bedding, cooking utensils, clothing, and approximately five hundred pounds of flour.

The Moulton family became a part of the James Grey Willie Handcart Company. It was an assignment that earned them a place in history. Among the five hundred Saints in the Willie Company were more than the usual number of elderly people. The company consisted of five wagons, twenty-four oxen, forty-five beef cattle, a tent for every twenty people, and 120 handcarts, one for every five people.

The ten-member Moulton family had two handcarts, one covered and one open. Thomas and Sarah pulled the covered cart. Baby Charles nestled on a pillow between the two youngest girls inside the cart. Eight-year-old Heber trailed along behind. A rope around his waist kept the lad from wandering. The older children pushed and pulled the open cart.

When the Willie Company left Camp Iowa the morning of July 15, 1856, to begin the thirteen hundred mile journey to Utah, the Saints couldn't know what lay in store. If they had, some might not have held on to their dream of joining Brigham Young in Zion. Knowing the peril, it's likely most would have set out anyway. They believed they would find the Kingdom of God with Brigham Young in Utah.

The journey started easily enough as the Saints pulled their handcarts across the prairie. Waving grasses, flowers, and wild fruit covered the plains. There were plenty of fish in the streams. Honey could be purchased from settlers as they passed. Milk was readily accessible from the cows they trailed. By August 11, 1856, when the Willie Company reached the Saints' winter headquarters at Florence, Nebraska, the green-wood handcarts were in bad shape. Willie's party repaired the carts that could be fixed and abandoned those too worn and deteriorated to be of further use.

As Willie prepared to depart from Florence, people who knew the trail cautioned against starting the journey so late in the season. Discussion was long and sometimes heated, but finally the Saints decided to press forward. Only one man voted against starting the venture. In mid-August Willie's company left eastern Nebraska with fully loaded carts, but short provisions none-the-less for the journey across plains and mountains that are now in Nebraska and Wyoming.

The plains' crossing was uneventful, but that quickly changed as the pioneers walked west. First they met a band of Indians whom they feared, but who turned out to be friendly. After trading for some trinkets, the immigrants pressed on only to come upon the bodies of other travelers who had been killed. The Saints gathered the mutilated bodies and buried them. Not many days later they heard of other attacks and deaths. The assaults weighed upon the hearts of the travelers and made them more vigilant. Even so raiding Indians or renegade whites stole many of their cattle, but there was no direct attack on the handcart company.

The Mormons, while devout in their religion, didn't prepare for life on the frontier. They had neither proper clothing and food, nor the abilities to live off the land. It seemed none of the company could kill a buffalo to eat, though they did use buffalo chips for fuel.

Early in September a buffalo stampede in central Nebraska at Wood River took the Willie Company cattle herd. Although the men in the party searched, they failed to recover about thirty animals. The loss meant more than short rations. The oxen pulled wagons so their disappearance meant handcarts had to be loaded with an additional measure of flour to lighten the loads for the remaining draft animals. The company also yoked the beef cattle and milk cows to help draw the wagons as they journeyed west.

The cattle pulled the supply wagons until they became too starved to handle the load. Then Thomas Moulton spent the night butchering a cow for the entire party. Animals too weak to move wagons became meat and meager sustenance for the immigrants.

As they tramped west, the party ran short on provisions. Many people were ill and deaths occurred almost daily from cholera and the effects of a poor diet. They were only in western Nebraska by September 12, 1856, and provisions were desperately low when a party of LDS missionaries returning to Salt Lake City from their work in Europe overtook the Willie Company. Seeing the plight of the ill, travel-weary travelers, the missionaries promised to continue west to Salt Lake City and send relief.

Willie and his followers continued plodding west. The first frost chilled them September 15. Finally at the end of the month they reached Fort Laramie on the banks of the North Platte River, still five hundred miles from their destination. The company found buffalo robes and barrels of crackers left at Fort Laramie by the missionaries, but no flour to bolster their meager supply.

Undaunted despite warnings that it was too late in the season to leave the Fort for the trek across the mountains to Utah,

Willie's Company pushed on toward Zion. They left behind a trail of broken handcarts, clothing, bedding, personal items, and, sadly, their dead.

"Every death weakened our forces. In my hundred I could not raise enough men to pitch a tent when we camped," twenty-four-year-old John Chislett wrote in his journal as the group neared Independence Rock.

Leaders cut rations to conserve what food the party had as the Saints struggled through freezing streams, deep snows, piercing winds, and bitter temperatures. Snowflakes brushed their faces on October 19, the day leaders doled out the last of the flour that had been carefully rationed since Fort Laramie. Step after step they forced themselves on a few miles where they camped in the willows at the Three Crossings of the Sweetwater. That night eighteen inches of snow fell, scattering the last starving draft animals in the storm.

Dawn broke with five fewer people to struggle on toward Zion. The ground was hard-frozen so digging graves was an impossible task. Instead they buried the dead in a snowdrift. Two miles below Rocky Ridge on the Sweetwater, the storms grew so fierce the travelers could no longer continue. Before them lay Rocky Ridge with its layers of shelf rock that would jolt the handcarts they pushed and pulled as they climbed the stair-step face of the hillside. They made noon camp in the swirling snow and prayed relief from Salt Lake would arrive in time to save them.

John Chislett wrote:

Finally we were overtaken by a snowstorm which the shrill wind blew furiously about us. The snow fell several inches deep as we travelled along, but we dared not stop, for we had a sixteen-mile journey to make that day, and short of it we could not get wood and water.

As the company huddled and rested that noon in the swirling snow and bitter cold, a light wagon drove into camp from the west. Its occupants, Joseph A. Young and Stephen Taylor, had been spotted by some Willie Company members. Young and Taylor told the Willie party a train of supplies was on the way. The wagons sent from Salt Lake would provide relief. In addition to Willie's company, a party led by Edward Martin was headed to Zion. It was farther back on the trail, behind Willie. The people with Martin also suffered in the cold and went to bed at night with no food to ease the ache in their empty bellies.

"More welcome messenger never came from the courts of glory than these young men were to us," Chislett wrote.

The missionaries told Willie to push on because there were fifteen hundred emigrants to be rescued and the sixteen loads of provisions on the way from Fort Bridger would not last long.

As the Saints made the long, difficult, seemingly endless climb out of the Sweetwater Valley and up Rocky Ridge, it was bitter cold. They slipped and slid in the snow on the rocks and many frosted their hands, feet, and faces because they didn't have proper clothing for the frigid temperatures.

Coming over Rocky Ridge, a kindly old woman held Heber Moulton's hand as he trailed behind the handcart, with his rope around his waist. The act saved his right hand, but his unprotected left hand froze in the sub-zero weather. The flesh dropped off his fingers to the first joint and it eventually became necessary to saw off the blackened bones.

Willie and his people trudged down the long valley between Rocky Ridge and Rock Creek. Miserable in the cold, they were starving and so ill they had no energy left to grieve the deaths of their friends and relatives. As the barely warm sun started to dip below the distant cliffs west of the camp, several covered wagons appeared. The news spread like wild-fire.

Chislett wrote, "Shouts of joy rent the air; strong men wept till (sic) tears ran freely down their furrowed and sun-burnt cheeks. . . . Restraint was set aside in the general rejoicing, and as the brethren entered our camp, the sisters fell upon them and deluged them with kisses."

The Willie Company was in a place that had neither shelter nor wood and the members had not had anything to eat for two days. They were literally freezing and starving to death. The relief helped, but was too late for many. Nine people died that night.

The following day, October 22, 1856, Willie's party camped

under the cliffs at Rock Creek, on the brink of South Pass, where an additional fifteen people died. The next night the Saints built a bonfire to thaw the ground. They wanted to dig a mass grave for the people who had perished during the day. Thirteen are buried in a common, oval-shaped grave, beneath the silent granite cliffs, and near the rushing Rock Creek. Two others lie in a separate tomb.

Two days later, on October 24, the company reached South Pass itself and they could see Oregon Buttes to the west. More importantly they found flour and plenty of wood on hand for their needs. Daily after that as they trudged west, the Saints met relief wagons sent by Brigham Young.

For many the long walk ended at Fort Bridger November 2, 1856, when the Willie Company arrived to find fifty teams sent from the settlement north and south of Salt Lake to haul them the remainder of the way. Some Saints continued to walk defiantly and eventually dragged their battered handcarts into Salt Lake in late November.

The Moultons gladly accepted the offer of a ride. At the foot of Little Mountain in Emigration Canyon, Uncle Custley met the wagon-load of Moultons with a supply of bread and butter sandwiches. Finally, about noon November 9, 1856, the wagons filled with starving handcart immigrants stopped in front of the old tithing office in Salt Lake City.

Charles was a mere infant skeleton, so weak and frail that no one expected him to live. A pillow supported him. When held up to the sun people could see right through his pitiful little body, some sources reported. People came from all around to see him, and to give Sarah Moulton warm clothing for her children.

The blessing given the Moultons before they left England became a reality. Not one member of the family perished on the hazardous journey. Through their faith and prayers and the tender care they gave him, the youngest member of the family at the time of their exodus to America grew to manhood. The Moulton family fanned out and grew, with three additional children born after arrival in Utah.

The hardships endured by the Moultons and others in the Mormon handcart companies of 1856, were probably the most severe of any faced during the western migration. Records show between sixty-two and seventy-seven members of the Willie Handcart Company died, as did an additional 135 to 150 members of the Edward Martin Handcart Company that was several days behind Willie.

Dreams and Yellow Roses

We are on the summit now—I can see Jackson Hole.

—Maggie McBride, 1896

Death and destruction crashed into the senses of sixteen-year-old Henrie May just north of Shelley, Idaho, as dawn spread over the land in June 1896. Henrie often did a man's share of the work and trailed his father's cattle from Rockland to Blackfoot, Idaho, but the sight of mangled horses' bodies rocked him and shocked him.

Henrie and his parents, James Ira and Ann (Henrie) May, were headed to a new home in Wyoming. Two years before, James, with a friend and a pack horse, rode throughout the West searching for a place to claim homestead land. He had two motivations. The land where he was living at Rockland,

Idaho, had an apt name because there certainly were plenty of rocks to make farming difficult. A staunch member of the Church of Jesus Christ of Latter-day Saints, he also was answering the call of the church to settle new areas.

On his exploratory trip, James rode his horse out of Idaho and dropped into the mountain-ringed Jackson Hole north of Jackson's Lake. May followed the Snake downstream. He found a few families settled in the southern end of the valley, bachelors who'd claimed homestead land along Flat Creek and the Gros Ventre River, and what he was looking for: an area of thick, tall sagebrush that was sheltered by a large, pine-covered butte.

The butte's name is Blacktail. At one flank the Gros Ventre mountains slope to the valley floor and the Gros Ventre River meanders across the land. Near the other flank the glacier-covered Tetons rise. The view was and still is spectacular, but James May wasn't interested in scenery. He wanted land. He sought rich productive soil and the thick sagebrush clearly indicated that was the case.

James took note of the nearby Gros Ventre River that could be diverted to provide water for crops. He eyed the tall, straight timber near the Snake River. He knew it would do for building a home and other necessities of the ranch he dreamed of creating.

With a satisfied nod James mounted his horse and returned to his Idaho home. His initial excursion into Jackson Hole showed him enough to make the decision to pull up his Idaho roots and head for Wyoming. It took two years to raise the necessary finances for the move. By the end of that time he had a herd of cattle and horses, five hundred dollars in his pocket, and plans for prosperity in his mind.

In June of 1896 James, Ann, and Henrie May packed their belongings for the move to Wyoming. They crammed as much as they could into their two wagons, but the horses that pulled them could only handle so much weight and they left behind many things, including an organ. Henrie found room in one wagon for his fiddle and slipped his harmonica into his pocket.

James drove one wagon, Ann the other. Henrie took charge of the livestock. Besides the teams pulling the wagons the Mays also had several other horses, a herd of forty-five head of cattle, part of which may have belonged to other families, and a crate or two of chickens.

Just north of Shelley the Mays camped near the railroad tracks they had been following. All was well when they crawled into their makeshift beds that June night. They awoke to tragedy.

Henrie May recalled the morning this way:

Father walked up on the track and he says "well, Buttons [is] dead." That was a saddle horse, colt I was breaking and I thought I fed him a little too much grain the night before and he just bloted maybe and I didn't pay any more attention. . . . The train had run into a big gray stallion killed him and evidently after they got him loose they steamed up and had a lot of power on and when they came on down they hit our horses. . . . There were seven head and there was two saddle horses in the bunch and there was a bay mare and we had two horses on a wagon and we had two wagons. The team was Snip and Bill. . . . The bay horse [Bill] had his legs broke off just below the knees and the Snip horse was up the track toward the Falls, they just riddled him. The blue saddle horse was just below, towards Shelley. My father had to hoof it up to St. Anthony and get the section crew and they came down and shot this one horse. He had his legs broke just below the knees. There were seven head of the horses killed. Then all we had left was a clyde [clydesdale] stallion and a little bay mare that was heavy with [foal]. We had to get some more horses before we could move.

James returned to Rockland for horses, part of which he rounded up from a herd he'd left behind earlier. The organ also served a purpose. Its sale provided money so James could buy even more horses. It took nearly a month for May to return to the site of the train tragedy. When May trailed the new horses in to his wife's camp, a handful of shirt-tail relatives accompanied him, including Charles and Mariah (Lish) Allen. Allen and May were cousins. The Allens had five of their children along as they embarked on a new life in Wyoming with the Mays. Roy and Maggie McBride completed the party. Although not any relation to the Mays or the Allens, they had been neighbors in Rockland.

Mary Ann Allen, the eldest daughter of Charles and Maria, and her husband of two months were also in the traveling party. Mary Ann went by the nickname Nan and in later years became Aunt Nan to both relatives and non-relatives. She was born April 25, 1877, in Calls Fort, Utah, and married James Budge April 25, 1895, at Rockland. Besides the necessary items to establish a home, Mary Ann had in her wagon a slip taken from her favorite yellow rose bush at the old home in Rockland.

The McBrides drove the last wagon. Roy McBride settled with his family in Rockland when he was only sixteen. Maggie McBride, christened Mary Margaret Robinson, was born March 5, 1868, at Mishoppen, Pennsylvania, the daughter of Cuthbert B. and Eunice E. Robinson. She had four sisters and a brother. The family came west when her father helped build the Union Pacific Railroad back in the 1860s.

Maggie chronicled the trip from June 22, 1896, until arrival in Jackson Hole in July. At age twenty-eight, Maggie was a big woman who liked to ride her horse Waif and to shoot rabbits. "I have never seen so many rabbits before, there are trails all over," she wrote. From Rockland to Eagle Rock [now Idaho Falls] where the four families gathered, traveling was uneventful. Maggie's diary is full of references to the pesky mosquitos that "just about ate us up."

Maggie and Roy McBride had a wagon and two saddle horses, which enabled Maggie to ride and avoid the rough journey on a bouncing wagon seat that the other women endured. Her journal provides a glimpse into the trek across the mountain:

July 3, 1896. We are all packed ready to go. The men are catching the horses. The mosquitos are awful. So thick I can neither read nor write. They leave at dark but start up at sunrise. We have to have breakfast before dawn. Now it is noon and we are at the Driggs Post Office, still fighting mosquitos. Charley is having his wagon fixed. Some of the men went to look at a ranch to take, but they did not like it. . . . We left there about six o'clock and drove until dusk.

Roy McBride with several wolf pelts. Some sources say McBride's hunting largely contributed to the demise of the wolf in the wild in Jackson Hole. (Photo Credit: Teton County Historical Center)

We got stuck in the mud. Were still stuck when Valdez [the Allen's son] came and said there was a deer back a ways. Roy left the team stuck in the mud and went flying after the deer. We had camped when he caught up to us again. He did not get the deer.

The Fourth of July 1896 found the travelers in Victor, Idaho, which was in the midst of the Independence Day celebration.

Henrie May said:

We came through Victor and everyone was gathering for a celebration there. . . . They had a store and some log cabins were there and there was a saloon there. I told them we furnished the parade that day coming through Victor. We had on some of our wagons some chickens and . . . McBrides were the last wagon and they picked up the eggs that fell out of the wagon and finally got enough so they could make a custard.

Winding their way up the mountain proved to be a difficult task. Often the wagons were too heavy for the single teams of horses to pull, making it necessary to double team. Instead of two horses pulling, four or even six had to draw the wagons up the steep mountain. While most of the men and women walked up the mountain, Maggie rode Waif. The mosquitos were vicious. The company traveled in the morning and camped in the afternoon. That gave the men, and often Maggie, time to hunt.

It took a great effort to reach Teton Pass summit. The travelers found it necessary to run four or six horse hitches on their wagons while climbing a trail that was just a rough track at best.

Maggie wrote:

July 6, Monday: Two weeks ago today we left home. Come about two miles, then doubled on three wagons, brought them to the top of the mountain, but had to put three teams on before we reached the top. The men went back after the other wagons, while we fixed dinner. We had tea made from snow water. We are on the summit now—I can see Jackson Hole.

The journey down into Jackson Hole was just as trying. Wagons had to be rough-locked, with poles stuck through the wheels to keep them from turning and heavy trees tied on the back to drag and act as a brake. Some people rough-locked their wagons by using a chain to keep the wheels from turning. Those tactics were necessary to keep the wagons from moving too quickly down the mountain and running up against the back legs of the horses.

On top of the effort to slowly and laboriously get the wagons first up one side and then down the other side of the mountain, Roy McBride lost his shotgun. There was nothing to do but look for it. He did and found it in the rough track they'd left on the west side of the pass.

The night of July 7, 1896, the party camped along a stream, probably near the present-day town of Wilson. Ann May told Henrie to take a bucket and get her some water. When Henrie dipped the bucket into the stream he spotted some large yellow-bellied trout. Though he may have been doing a man's work, Henrie was a youth and he loved to fish. It wasn't long before he had his hand in the water and was sliding it up along the back of the fish, tickling it, and then hooking the trout by the gills and throwing it to the stream bank.

When Henrie returned to camp, trout filled his bucket rather than the water his mother had requested. It didn't take her long to remind him the true reason why he went to the creek. Henrie fetched the requisite pail of water.

The musically-gifted Henrie spent evening hours sitting on the wagon tongue playing his harmonica and violin. The mournful sounds could have been an echo of his longing for a home he'd left behind—one he likely would never see again. His music blended with the steady hum of mosquitos.

The second day in Jackson Hole the travelers explored and relaxed. Maggie told the story this way:

> *July 8:* Part of the crowd went to a lake fishing, [Phelps Lake] four miles from camp. We went horseback. There was no road. We went through timber and rocks, when we got near the lake we tied our horses and walked. Roy struck out up the lake through fallen timber, underbrush and boulders, I followed him. When I got where there was good fishing I was tired out. Roy caught nine, I caught five, then Roy made a fire on a rock, and fried some fish. Ate our dinner; then struck out for camp, but Roy had to fish some more, so I came home with Jim and Nan, we went flying. . . . Mosquitos worse than ever.

Finally on July 9 the party was at the wide torrent of the Snake River. There the men tried to cut a deal with ferry owner Bill Menor. They attempted to trade a bucket of lard, flour, and cured pork for the right to cross the river on his ferry. Menor wasn't interested. The price was a buck fifty per wagon to cross on the ferry, take it or leave it. The travelers coughed up the money, but only paid for the wagons and the people. The horses and cattle had to swim.

The journey ended in the cottonwoods along the Gros Ventre River at the south end of Blacktail Butte. The families had arrived. It was time to begin carving a life in the valley.

On July 24, 1896, Jim Lannigan and Jim Simpson, two of the many bachelors who made their homes in the valley for the previous several years, welcomed the party to Jackson Hole. "Of course they were interested in the girls," Maggie said.

Those bachelors did more than visit the daughters of Charles and Mariah Allen, they also opened their homes to the newly-arrived contingent. Though they intended to claim homestead land and build cabins, the four families had other priorities upon arrival in Jackson Hole.

It was late July in a country known for short summers. They had to cut and stack hay to feed their stock during the rapidly-approaching winter. There wasn't time to construct cabins, too.

The men helped Martin "Slough Grass" Nelson harvest his hay. Their assistance to Nelson gave them the "privilege" of gleaning around the swamps for what hay they would need to get their stock through the winter. Wearing hip boots they waded into the wet area where the "hay" was growing. The pioneers waited for the wettest places of the swamp to freeze,

Slough Grass Nelson had an early homestead in Jackson Hole and often let newcomers harvest "hay" on his place. (Photo Credit: Teton County Historical Center)

then sharpshod the teams by putting shoes on the horses that had sharp points on the bottom. The men wrapped chains around the mower wheels for traction. It was possible to harvest the forage, but the men cut the hay so late it never had a chance to cure and soon turned black. Nevertheless, it provided nourishment for the cows during that first winter.

Slough Grass had two cabins connected with a breezeway and winter found the Mays living in one cabin. Roy and Maggie McBride lived with Jim Lannigan, while Jim and Nan Budge and the Allen family lived in the home of Johnny Carnes.

Before winter struck, the men started the process necessary to claim homestead land in Jackson Hole. To comply with the law they had to work the land and live on it at least six months every year. Cabin construction started, but it wasn't finished that first year.

The May house when meals were thirty-five cents. Ann May seated on porch. (Photo Credit: Clark and Veda Moulton Collection)

When summer rolled around again James May staked a homestead claim east of Blacktail Butte and hauled logs from the butte for a two-room cabin. He only stayed in the cabin long enough to prove up on the first parcels of land, then he bought a big pre-cut frame house and built it a half mile farther north and on the east side of the lane between the homesteads.

Carpenters sent from the company that sold it to May erected the new house. As the builders finished the job they ran into the determination of a woman. Ann May wanted a blue roof on her new home, but the crew had a supply of yellow paint. The crew refused to apply the blue paint Ann bought, but following heated arguments with the woman of the family, they mixed her blue with their yellow making a bilious green for the roof. Ann then used the remaining concoction on everything in and around the premises. Cupboards, chairs, vanities, and doors all turned green.

The family needed a house, but a barn for the livestock was equally important. James May built a huge log barn and a large granary. The barn was about fifteen logs high. James cut the logs at Timber Island a few miles northwest of the homestead, where the trees grew straight, tall, and uniform in size. He hauled many logs on a hard-wheeled wagon, two or three at a time because they were green and heavy for the horses to pull. May and his neighbors did much of the barn-building work in wintertime when crossing the frozen Snake River wasn't difficult. The men also cut and hauled some timber during the summer.

At the time of construction for May and his neighbors, the only Snake River crossing was at Menor's Ferry. The frugal homesteaders could afford the then fifty-cent fee to cross the ferry on the way for timber, but found it hard to come up with enough to pay for every return crossing. The men loaded their logs on the wagon and then approached the river bank. There they forced the horses into the river and headed upstream so the energy of the water pushed the logs, which acted as a natural raft, across the current. It was a quick and dangerous trip, but the men did it as many as twenty times just for the timber necessary to build the May barn.

Jim Budge staked his claim south of May and built a one-room log house with a window, a door, and a sod roof. Though it no doubt filled the requirements of the Homestead Act, the cabin was less than perfect. When it rained the dirt roof leaked a steady stream of muddy water, so that during the early years on the homestead Aunt Nan found it necessary to stash the two babies she had after arriving in Jackson Hole under the oil cloth-covered table to keep them somewhat clean and dry. After the rain stopped, it could take a couple of hours for the house roof to quit leaking.

Aunt Nan brightened her life with a reminder of home, however. She planted the slip from the yellow rose bush she brought from Rockland. It flourished. Soon her neighbors had yellow roses growing in their yards as well. As the men worked to forge a life in a new land, the women struggled to make a home. The men had their dreams of prosperity. The women had their yellow roses.

After Jim Budge proved up on his initial 160-acre claim, he took an eighty-acre timber and mineral claim across the lane. There he built a log home and barn. He moved the little home-stead cabin down next to the hill. Its use was as a pig pen. Another smaller log cabin situated right behind the kitchen door in the willows served as a milk and cooling room for meat.

Charley Allen lived that first winter in the Johnny Carnes home, then he headed north toward Moran to claim home-stead land. Roy and Maggie McBride homesteaded on Flat Creek, closer to the present-day town of Jackson and the National Elk Refuge.

The Mays and the Budges were the first homesteaders in the area that became known as Mormon Row. Many of the early settlers in the valley, including those who had been living in the south end of the park in 1896, were members of the Church of Jesus Christ of Latter-day Saints.

Those who settled near Blacktail Butte claimed land along a straight lane. Their homes were about a half mile apart, all in a straight line. Most, but not all, of the homesteaders along that three mile lane were Mormons, so it naturally followed that the lane's name is Mormon Row. That appellation first was an epithet used by people not living on the lane; today it has more reverence attached.

By 1900 the Mays and the Budges had cattle herds to care for. In the summertime the cows could be turned loose to graze along the Gros Ventre, but during the winter they had to be kept close to home. To survive the harsh winters they needed the hay laboriously cut and stacked as part of an annual ritual.

In those early years, many Jackson Hole elk migrated over the passes headed for the Green River country to winter where the snow wasn't so deep and where the temperature wasn't so cold. But, not all the elk left and that created problems for set-tlers who had to protect their haystacks from the wild animals. It just wouldn't do to have a herd of elk get into a stack needed for the survival of the cattle and horses that the families depended on for food and transportation.

James May solved his problem of elk in the hay by sending son Henrie, then in his late teens, to spend the night in the stack standing guard. The fodder provided at least minimal insulation against the frigid temperatures and snow that swept the valley.

Henrie recalled his experience this way:

> I sat in the hay stacks and fought elk out of the hay stacks at that time and that wasn't very comfortable. I had big long German socks. If you remember what they look like, they come clear to your crotch and I had a tent, a little tent that we put on the hay stack right out on the bench. . . . I'd put on skis and push them [the elk] back into the timber and then come back to bed. I had an old 45-70 [rifle] that I held there beside my bed and I'd shoot it off a few times, but they didn't pay much attention. They would just run off a little ways and then come back.

Henrie entertained with his harmonica or fiddle when the family first made its wagon trek into Jackson Hole and after settling at Blacktail Butte he often played for a dance in the valley. One night he went into the small but growing town of Jackson on just such an excursion and returned to his haystack post late in the night.

Henrie used a ladder to climb to his tent atop the stack. On that night he burrowed into the sweet smelling hay, left the burning lantern hanging from a post nearby, and began his elk watch. But the day had been long, the music relaxing, and the hay bed was comfortable. Before long Henrie slept soundly. He didn't hear the elk pushing and crowding to get at the hay, but awoke as the sun's blush turned the Gros Ventre range the color of a pale pink rose. Henrie saw churned snow where the elk milled during the darkness. His ladder and lantern were missing.

Henrie followed the tracks as they headed away from the stack and toward the ridge, but he didn't find the lantern until after dark that second day. As Henrie started his next moonlight vigil, an old bull elk returned for a second helping of sweet hay. According to family legend, the lantern dangled from his antlers. Some say it was still lit, though that seems to be too much of a tall tale to believe.

Henrie combined his hay-watching duty with his musical gift as he traveled to dances at one end of the valley or the other to make the strings of his violin sing. Once bachelor

Some Hereford bulls Henrie May purchased in Ogden, Utah, standing in front of the J.H. May home. (Photo Credit: Clark and Veda Moulton Collection)

mailman Jim Lannigan invited Henrie to go to Moran on the regular route. In Jackson Hole's early days Lannigan skied from Jackson to Moran with the postal dispatches. In later years a mailman using a horse and wagon made the deliveries. In both instances the mail carrier made a stop at the Mormon Row community to rest and prepare for the next leg of the journey. On one such stop Lannigan told Henrie to strap his fiddle on his back and prepare for the ski journey to the small community farther north.

Though it was twenty-some miles to Moran from Mormon Row, Henrie didn't hesitate at the chance to see something besides cattle, elk, and hay. The long-legged mailman used eight-foot long homemade skis and a long pole to help propel himself along, making it a chore for Henrie to keep up. The boy arrived at Moran completely exhausted.

Lannigan always spent a couple of days in Moran before starting the return trip and on this occasion, since Henrie had his fiddle, those in the community quickly organized a party. There was only one lone Indian woman living at the upper end of the valley, but the lack of femininity didn't dampen the celebration staged in one bachelor's cabin. The men soon raised a swirl of dust by stomping their feet and swinging each other about. A jug of hooch, lots of boiled elk meat, biscuits, and beans—made by the woman of course—livened the gathering.

The following morning Lannigan shouldered his sack of mail and Henrie packed his fiddle as they strapped on their skis. They made the twenty-five mile return trip from Moran in about four hours.

The fiddle was in use again a couple of years later when Henrie spied a pretty young girl named Hadden Maria (Hattie) Wood visiting some of her family in Jackson Hole. The two young people became acquainted and later married. James May gave Henrie land adjacent to his homestead and another generation of Jackson Hole ranchers was soon on the way. Henrie and Hattie had eight children: Clifton, Leland, Murland, Lester, Veda, Wayne, Ada, and Arva. In later years some of those children also played music and ranched on Mormon Row.

The Henrie and Hadden May home where Veda May Moulton was born and spent her childhood. (Photo Credit: Clark and Veda Moulton Collection)

Henrie and Hadden May. (Photo Credit: Veda Moulton Collection)

A Poor Man's Legacy

Those two barns are typical mountain country barns. They represent a culture.
—Jackson Artist Conrad Schwiering, 1984 referring
to the T.A. and John Moulton barns.

Thomas Alma Moulton claimed a homestead on Mormon Row in 1907 when he was twenty-four years old. His cousin George Jr. made the application for the land, but when the filing was close to being granted, George changed his mind and offered the land to Alma.

Alma was the eldest of eleven children born to Charles and Rhoda Moulton. Charles, the infant on the Willie Company crossing with the Mormon handcart companies, lived his early life in Utah and eventually married Rhoda Francis Duke. In 1895, he and his youngest brother George Sr. filed homestead claims in Idaho's Teton Basin. They built a log cabin for

George, splitting shingles out of water-soaked blocks of wood. In the spring they plowed some ground and planted oats, then they returned to Utah for their families.

On the Fourth of July 1895, Charles and Rhoda took their children and left Utah for Teton Basin. It was an unnerving trip for Rhoda. Bannock Indians, furious about new Wyoming game hunting laws that they said restricted their freedom and violated their treaty rights, were riding throughout the country. A number of them clashed with law officers in the Hoback country of western Wyoming.

Charles Alma Moulton came to America with Mormon immigrants in 1856 and survived the Willie Handcart disaster. (Photo Credit: Clark Moulton Collection)

There was no truth to early reports of massacre in Jackson Hole, but news was slow in coming and the Moultons moving through Idaho had warnings to be on the lookout. Rhoda, used to the settled life in a Utah town, felt fear twist her gut as the wagons rolled north. Her trepidation was unnecessary. The Indians didn't bother the travelers, or anyone else for that matter.

Other worries about her safety added to the emotional tension and mosquitoes were a constant source of aggravation. At

Bear Lake the Moultons met a one-horse buggy being driven by two women. As the wagons passed on the narrow trail, the buggy tipped over, further jangling Rhoda's nerves, which were already on edge.

At Eagle Rock, the huge Idaho canal had to be crossed. There were no bridges, so the family forded the deep, powerful water as Rhoda sat upon the wagon seat huddled in fear and trepidation. Though some people thrive on adventure and danger, Rhoda shrank from the tension. She was immensely relieved when eventually the Moultons arrived at the Idaho homestead where they lived in George's cabin until Charles could build a house.

The family had two cows and a pig for milk and meat. Charles raised grain to sell for groceries such as flour, sugar, pickles, molasses, and salt. Rhoda harvested from the land. Fruit including huckleberries, choke cherries, service berries, and grapes that grew in the wild became jelly and syrup to flavor the staples.

Charles and Rhoda's son, Thomas Alma, was twelve years old the summer the family moved to Idaho. He did a man's work on his father's homestead for the next six years, before starting the lonely, isolated work of an Idaho sheepherder. He herded the flocks until 1907 when his cousin George Jr. informed him of the opportunity to claim a section of homestead land in Jackson Hole.

With his younger brother John, and neighbor Thomas Perry, Alma saddled his horse and left the family holdings in Idaho headed for Jackson Hole. There on September 9, 1907, Alma filed on a homestead his cousin had chosen earlier. John took a claim adjacent. Both were on the straight lane known as Mormon Row.

Perry made his own claim for free land across the lane to the south and east. The three then returned to Idaho to herd sheep and Alma served a mission for the LDS church. It wasn't until 1908 that they returned to Jackson to begin the process of proving up on their claims.

They hauled logs from the slightly upraised area a few miles northwest of their land that they called Timber Island. There pine grew straight and tall. The logs became fences as the Moultons worked their land in one common area. A year later another Moulton brother, Wallace, joined them, claiming a section of ground and fencing it with the rest.

The next couple of winters found Alma in Idaho herding sheep, but during the summers he was in Jackson Hole making improvements to the homestead and fulfilling the residency requirements of the Homestead Act. Alma built a fourteen by eighteen foot log cabin. Poles laid side-by-side and covered with sod formed a roof. The dirt that was already there formed the floor and a door was the only opening. The structure was crude, but adequate for the bachelor Alma as he worked his land.

Finally in 1912 Alma moved permanently to his homestead. He was no longer a bachelor, having married Lucile Blanchard in 1910. He also was the father of a son, Clark Alma, born shortly before relocation to Wyoming. The trip from Idaho to Jackson Hole was in a wagon pulled by the family's team of horses, Don and Saylor. They trailed Sally, Lucile's buckskin mare, and a cow and calf. The five animals and the wagon represented their stake as Alma and Lucile started their homesteading life together on Mormon Row.

Tears rained down Lucile's cheeks to fall in drops on the dirt floor as she walked into the one-room homestead cabin carrying Clark in her arms. Dirt had sifted down from the pole roof to cover the crude furniture with a substantial icing. Mice scurried back to their hiding places at the intrusion. Although it was theirs, the cabin, actually the entire homestead, needed much work to become a home. It was not nearly so nice as the dwelling she had left in Idaho.

The original T.A. Moulton homestead house. (Photo Credit: Harley Moulton Collection)

One of the first inconveniences was a lack of water. Like others at Grovont—the official community name for Mormon Row—Alma routinely loaded barrels on a wagon and headed for the Gros Ventre River to fill the containers. Alma hauled water for domestic use at the house during all seasons and for the livestock in the winter.

Although the earliest settlers at Grovont, led by the Mays, engineered and dug ditches for irrigation water for their crops and stock water for their animals, most didn't dig wells until many years after they arrived. The ditches were fine in the summer for providing stock water for cattle, horses, and chickens, but when the frigid temperatures of winter enveloped the valley, the ditches froze solid.

During winter, by far the longest season of the year sometimes lasting seven or eight months, the men found it necessary to harness teams to wagons and drive them to the river to get water. It, like feeding the animals, was a routine that never varied and one chore that the homesteaders could never forget.

A shelter for the animals was as important to the family as a house and water. Horses and cattle provided transportation and food. Without them survival at Grovont would have been nearly impossible.

Like others of the homestead era, Alma Moulton had visions of a ranch and prosperity someday. But when he needed a barn for his livestock, he had to rely on his own brute strength and careful craftsmanship. He was a poor man with a young family and dreams of a better future for his children. The barn he built is a poor man's legacy.

The faithful draft horses, Don and Saylor ready for work in front of the barn that sheltered them from the harsh elements of Jackson Hole. (Photo Credit: Clark and Harley Moulton)

Alma's barn is of a style common to the era and is not particularly unique in any way. It would be decades before he completed the barn, and part of a century before it would become a symbol of America and the struggle and perseverance of a homesteader.

Alma started construction of his barn in 1913. It would be a warm place for horses Don and Saylor who pulled the family wagon from Teton Basin in Idaho. They faithfully pulled the wagon to the Gros Ventre for water and found themselves hitched to varying types of farm equipment to till the soil, plant crops, and reap the harvest. Don and Saylor were nearly as important to the family's survival as Alma himself. They deserved shelter.

Alma cut and hauled lodgepole pine from Timber Island using the team for the skidding work. Then he carefully trimmed and notched the logs, laying them twelve rows up in a rectangular section that was eighteen feet wide and twenty-four feet long. The roof was flat, made with slabs Alma got at the sawmill in the nearby town of Kelly.

The T.A. Moulton Barn. (Photo Credit: Candy Moulton)

When finished the shelter looked like a big box, but it protected the animals well enough for the time being. Alma stacked bundles of grain on the flat roof for years to seal it and to shed water and snow. Alma barely had enough money for the nails for that first box-like section. It would be a decade before more work could be done and take more than twenty years in all to complete his barn.

In 1928, Alma and son Clark, who was then sixteen-years-old, added five more rows of logs to make a hayloft and a half pitch roof on the original box-like structure. In 1934, they added a lean-to for horses used on the mail run between Jackson and Moran. By 1939, the family's livestock had outgrown the available space, so Clark and his eighteen-year-old brother Harley built a hog barn on the north side, topping it with a tin roof. The family dairy operation took place in the original center section of the barn and horses used the south side lean-to.

The finished product was not only functional, it eventually became one of the picturesque old buildings in Jackson Hole, a magnet for painters and photographers intent on capturing a bit of Americana.

In the long run, considerably more money has been made from the sale of photographs and art prints of the T.A. Moulton barn than it cost to construct the whole building. The barn in Grand Teton National Park isn't unique in its design, but the Tetons rising behind it, the weathered wood and the surrounding meadow make for good photographs and paintings. It aged gracefully, and time turned the native timber a rich brown. Inside, spiders spin webs where horses and cattle once lived.

Over the years, photographs of the Moulton Barn have

The T.A. Moulton Barn. (Photo Credit: Candy Moulton)

graced hundreds—perhaps thousands—of cards, magazines, jigsaw puzzles, and newspapers. It is featured on the Jackson State Bank credit card, many book jackets, and the Hollywood classic *Spencer's Mountain* used the barn for location shots.

The Moultons watched in amusement when actor Henry Fonda arrived at their barn one day during filming for that picture. In the first stall on the south side of the barn Fonda struggled to milk the cow Blossom, a chore any self-respecting homesteader's son could do by the time he was eight.

The family built the barn sturdily, reinforcing it at several points to withstand the massive amounts of snow that fall in Jackson Hole. It is a structure pieced together by a homesteading family according to present need and the condition of the pocketbook. Other structures, including a chicken house, corrals, chute, and dipping vat, complete the picture of the homestead.

Alma and Lucile had a son when they moved to Grovont and over the next dozen years they added to it with daughters Melba, June, Rhoda Elizabeth (Betty), Helen, and son Harley.

A frame house soon replaced the crude cabin providing a better place for Lucile to raise her children. The birth of June in 1916 heralded a tough time for the family. Her home entrance to the world took place during a snow storm. Wallace Moulton's wife, Elizabeth, helped care for Lucile, the new baby, and the two older children, Clark and Melba.

The family paid little attention to Elizabeth's bad cough. Within three weeks the children had whooping cough. The disease was particularly hard on the three-week old June who barely survived, but by fall the two elder children were running and playing on the homestead and June was certain to live.

Although Lucile gladly accepted help from her neighbors and relatives during that period of sickness, during her lifetime it was more likely that she would be the one offering comfort and aid. She served as midwife for the births of at least twenty-two children on Mormon Row, often staying a few days after the birth of a baby to assist the mother with other children or simply to ease the burden of a new life. Rain or snow, whenever someone in need approached Lucile, she left her family and hurried down the lane to offer help, taking blankets, diapers, or food as the case warranted.

From the earliest days when the Moultons came to America as part of the Mormon handcart contingent, they were deeply religious. Lucile and Alma both served the LDS church for many years. She was Relief Society president for twenty-six years and he was the church Bishop on Mormon Row for twenty-nine years. They firmly believed in the teachings of the church and were self-reliant, always putting the family first. Although they knew the church would help them if they were in need, the Moultons adhered to the philosophy of "chasing your own rabbits" and not relying on others to provide for them.

As part of his responsibility to the church, Alma went to the small white building standing midway on the lane early every Sunday to start the fire. Sitting by the pot-bellied stove waiting for his little congregation to arrive, Alma bowed his head and studied lessons from the Bible and the Book of Mormon.

The first years the Moultons lived at Grovont, life was particularly hard. They had no irrigation system so they dry-farmed the land until the late 1920s, trusting that adequate natural moisture would come to make a crop. But the rain didn't always fall and after one particularly dry summer, Alma had little feed for the forty head of cattle he had struggled nearly twenty years to acquire. He bought what hay he could afford at fifty dollars a ton, but money was scarce and the amount of hay obtained not adequate for a long winter in Jackson Hole. Before the spring grass turned green, Alma was out cutting willows and quaker trees to feed his cattle. A little straw and oats supplemented that fodder.

After that experience, on September 25, 1929, Alma filed for an irrigation water right out of Mud Spring, a tributary of Ditch Creek at the Gros Ventre River. It took seven years to get permit approval and to build ditches that would carry water to the Moulton land and other homesteads in the area.

Winter snowbanks covered the fences as the temperature plunged to forty and fifty degrees below zero. Every day men hauled water, fed their stock, and provided for their families. It was an unyielding cycle in a harsh climate. During the weeks between Thanksgiving and Christmas, the smell of baked goods drifted from homes along the Row as the women did their best to give joy to their children. They bustled about making Christmas presents: practical gifts like knitted socks, mittens, and scarves.

Alma, Wallace, and John headed up the Gros Ventre canyon to chop wood for the winter. On the final trip they always cut Christmas trees for the children to decorate with homemade ornaments, strings of popcorn, and colored paper.

The homesteaders marked Christmas with a special worship service at the little white church down the lane and a Christmas pageant at the school just next door. Produced by

T.A. and Lucile Moulton
(Photo Credit: Harley
Moulton)

the children and their teacher, the pageant was a gala affair highlighted by music and laughter, home-baked goodies the women provided, and a visit from Santa Claus.

As winter lay over the land, Alma hauled water for the house needs and the livestock, struggling through deep snow to feed his animals. Lucile spent her days and nights sewing clothing for her family and others in the area. Quilting was a favorite pastime with a section of the living room always brightened by the pieced top of the current project. Lucile sewed the top and then tacked it to a frame sitting atop the backs of four chairs. As the snow fluttered or came in fierce, blinding blizzards, she sat by the fire, deftly pulling her needle up and down through the quilt layers stitching a design.

Lucile got wool from her father every summer to wash and store in sacks. During winter days and nights the children sat at her feet and picked the wool to clean it before she carded it for use in various creations.

Lucile's life on the homestead was not unlike that of any other woman of her generation. She had children and took care of them by cooking, sewing, cleaning, and nurturing as the need arose. She acted as doctor and nurse, and as a teacher if called upon. She raised a large garden that provided food and snacks, like carrots, fresh peas or turnips. She made soap, cured meat, canned fruit she picked wild and vegetables she raised in her garden, milked the cow if no one else was around to do so, and raised a few chickens for the eggs they laid or to stew with dumplings or noodles.

Like other women on the Row she sold butter and eggs, cream and milk to get a little cash money for the necessities that the family couldn't make or grow on its own. Primarily, however, the Moultons were independent and not reliant upon outside products for survival. Lucile seldom went to town, making the trip only once or twice a year for supplies, riding in a wagon or a horse-drawn sleigh with blankets over her knees and warmed rocks at her feet to ward off the cold.

When her domestic duties were done, and sometimes even if they weren't, she headed to the field with Alma to grub sagebrush from the land or help with the planting. With no machinery to do it, grain was sown by hand. Alma put seed in tubs and buckets and loaded them onto the lumber wagon. Lucile drove the team while Alma broadcast the seed. The children went along for the ride. Eventually Alma and his brothers saved enough money for a drill and other machinery.

Lucile's one real source of pleasure was her buckskin mare Sally, whom she loved to race across the fields. But when Alma needed another draft horse for the work on the homestead, he sold Sally. That act broke Lucile's heart and she never fully forgave him.

As the homestead became more productive, Alma decided

it was time to find a source of water. He enlisted the aid of Joe Pfeiffer, a bachelor homesteader in the area who was a hard worker and experienced to boot. Pfeiffer had helped many of the others along Mormon Row dig wells.

Pfeiffer came to the area from Butte, Montana, where he worked in the copper mines. He never married and had a distrust of most women, but liked kids to a point and usually had a little hard-tack candy in the pocket of his long-tailed denim jumper. After claiming his land and breaking the twenty acres necessary for him to get title to the ground, Pfeiffer didn't do much additional developing. His acreage produced an adequate amount of feed for his three white horses. Pfeiffer had a house and several out-buildings on his place. He once bought a milk cow, but the story goes that he sold the animal before he could get it home.

The well-digging was done by hand. The race-horse lean Pfeiffer used a short-handled shovel. To begin he rigged a wooden windlass over the well site. At first Pfeiffer threw the dirt aside, sifting it out of the hole in much the same way a badger or prairie dog digs. As he got deeper, big steel buckets strung on rope or cable through two strategically placed pullies, and powered by a single horse, lifted the dirt and rocks to the surface.

As Pfeiffer dug into the earth, he used split logs to crib the walls and keep the sides from caving in on him. The process was long and arduous. Usually well digging was a winter job because there was little else to do on the homestead. The surface of the ground shielded the digger from the winter cold, but the man or boy leading the horse to empty the buckets of dirt and rocks suffered from the exposure to frigid temperatures.

The wells ranged in depth, but most were about one hundred feet deep. Ironically, although Pfeiffer helped many Grovont homesteaders dig wells, he mined to a depth of more than 120 feet on a well for himself and never did hit water. Instead he diverted water in a ditch from the Gros Ventre during summer months and melted snow during the winter.

Some of the farmers hoisted the water they hit from the deep wells with the same windlass and horse used during digging operations. Saylor, the faithful old animal, was the draw horse for the Moultons, pulling a good many barrels of water out of the well for both the house and the cattle. Eventually the wells had hand pumps and even later the families added power pumps.

It would be years and take a natural disaster before the homesteaders could dispense with the routine of hauling stock water during the winter time and garden water during the summer from the Gros Ventre.

As the routine of life on the homestead passed, Alma made improvements to the house. The children attended school and started families of their own.

Alma and Lucile's eldest son, Clark, knew Veda May, granddaughter of James I. May, all his life, but finally he took more than a passing interest in her. "One night we went on a hayride. The moon was full and I planted a kiss on her and it was all over," he said.

Courting was done down the lane. Clark lived at the north end of the Row and Veda at the south end. He hitched a team to the sleigh and took a box of chocolates to go visit his girl.

Harley Moulton helped construct the final addition to the T.A. Moulton barn and started rearing his family on the homestead before its sale to the National Park Service in 1960. (Photo Credit: Harley Moulton Collection)

"Grandpa May had a dog that hated me with a passion. I had to carry a lot of jerky to get down there and needed more to get back," Clark said. His persistence paid off and the two married. They had three children, whom they reared on Mormon Row.

Clark's eldest sister Melba, also married a May as Veda's brother Lester would come courting from his end of the lane. The Mays lived on Mormon Row for a time with their five children, Lanny, Clara, Mary, Dick, and Bob. The other Moulton girls, June and Helen, left the area, and Betty died as a young girl.

Alma and Lucile's youngest son, Harley, left for a time to serve in the US Army Air Corps during World War II. He was with the first contingent of US troops sent into Japan after the armistice. When the war was over, he returned to Jackson Hole where in 1950 he married Flossie Woodward, whose grandparents homesteaded in the vicinity. Harley and Flossie settled on Alma's homestead where the first four of their five children, Dan, Ila, Steve, and Jerry, spent part of their childhood. They would have stayed to carry on the ranching tradition started by Alma and Lucile, but the land became the domain of the nation.

A Melting Pot

*I'll never forget it. When we got to the top of the pass we stopped there. . .
and I thought that was as near Heaven as I'd ever been.*

—Martha Riniker, 1977 talking of
her first view of Jackson Hole

By the time the Moultons established their homestead,
other families were developing land around Blacktail Butte.
Mormon Row, like much of America as the century turned,
became a melting pot. The Mays and the Moultons came from
England. George and John Riniker's family immigrated from
Switzerland, Hannes Harthoorn came from Holland, Dick Van
DeBrock was another young Dutchman. Others working soil in
the area were Jacobson Johnson, Joe Eggleston, a man named
Geck, Andy Cindle, Tom Murphy, Tom Perry, Andy Chambers,
Joe Pfeiffer, Joe Heniger, Billy Ireton, and of course the Scottish
Budges who had been with the first wave of settlers in 1896.

Without exception they came to Grovont for the opportunity to own ground. It was a place to put down roots and to raise families. Jackson Hole was just one spot in America where the European immigrants could build a new life where their children might have more than their ancestors had. Though the Moultons and Mays originally left their homeland to follow their faith, like the others who settled on Mormon Row they also sought independence and security. The first step in that quest was a home for the family and a barn for the livestock. Then thoughts turned to raising crops and cattle.

The men claiming homesteads at Grovont were a hardy lot used to making do for themselves and prepared to sacrifice and work hard for the greater goal of land ownership and the security that represented. In America a man could be his own boss and his future was before him ready to be shaped by the hard work of his calloused hands.

The families crossed America by one means or another to eventually arrive in Jackson Hole.

Among the earliest settlers there were Aunt Nan and James Budge. Nan had a zest for living and a fondness for animals. She took the problems of each day and capably handled them. Meanwhile, as Jim worked the land, he built up a solid herd of horses. Even though he didn't work on a breeding program, his animals often won the races at local rodeos.

One Budge horse was Aunt Nan's fishing partner. She rode to the Gros Ventre or the Snake River, and waded the horse into a likely looking spot. Then she'd stop the animal and, sitting upon its solid back, begin plying her bamboo fishing rod. The horse and the woman trolled up and down the river and before long plump fish filled the sack tied to the back of her saddle.

George Riniker was born in Dayton, Ohio, in 1885, the youngest child of a Swiss father and German mother. He had four sisters and an older brother. The story goes that George left home after a spanking from his sister Mary. He was seventeen and joined two friends in a journey from Dayton by boat, floating down the Ohio River. The three young men intended to go to Alaska Territory, but found themselves working at various ranch jobs on the way west.

The closest George ever got to the Alaskan frontier was the

winter he spent in Butte, Montana, with his brother, John. George eventually decided on Wyoming as a final destination, living first near Lander where he labored as a logger and ranch hand. He spent some time working in Jackson Hole for Mary Jane Wilson helping her with haying chores.

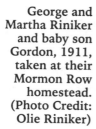

George and Martha Riniker and baby son Gordon, 1911, taken at their Mormon Row homestead. (Photo Credit: Olie Riniker)

Mary Jane was a widow who also had assistance from her brother, Nate Davis. During one of his visits to Jackson Hole, George Riniker met Mary Jane's younger sister, Martha Davis. It's not clear if George and Martha quickly fell in love or if their affection had a gradual birth. At any rate, George moved to Jackson Hole and the romance blossomed.

Martha was the daughter of John Amos and Susannah Davis. Susannah was a native of Piedmont, Italy, where she was born in 1850. She came to America with her family after their conversion to Mormonism. At age twenty she married Amos Davis Jr., a polygamist thirty years her senior. They had three children, Mary Jane, Lauretta, and Nathan, and adopted others left homeless when their parents died.

In 1877 Amos died and Susannah married one of the adopted children, John Amos Davis, who was ten years her senior. They had an additional five children, Tryphena, Naomi, Rhoda, John, and Martha, born August 27, 1891, in Huntington, Utah.

Mary Jane was the first of the family to come to Jackson Hole. She and her husband Ervin Wilson were with the initial wave of Mormon emigrants to move to the valley in 1889. At the time of their move, Mary Jane had one baby and in 1891, she gave birth to a daughter, Effie, who is credited as the first white child born in Jackson Hole.

Mary Jane's family continued to live in Desert Lake, Utah, and when her husband Ervin died, she asked her brother Nathan to come to Jackson Hole and help her with ranching chores. Nate's enthusiasm for the country resulted in his bringing his sisters, Lauretta, Naomi, and Rhoda. Finally in 1902 he sent money for the remainder of his family to make the move.

Susannah and Amos Davis were in their fifties and sixties as they loaded covered wagons, their younger children, including eleven-year-old Martha, and started the forty-two day trek from Price, Utah, to Jackson Hole. That trip etched itself into Martha's mind and in 1977 she clearly remembered her first glimpse of Jackson Hole on October 7, 1902.

"I'll never forget it. When we got to the top of the pass we stopped there . . . and I thought that was as near Heaven as I'd ever been. Oh, I just thought it was the most beautiful valley. It was so green and so pretty and after coming out of the desert, you can imagine what I thought about this place. And I never changed my mind," she told her grandson Olan Riniker.

Martha's family settled on what is now the South Park elk feeding grounds and she attended school in South Park. While living on that homestead she met George Riniker and the two married June 20, 1909, when Martha was seventeen and George was twenty-four.

George supported his new bride by working on the Jackson Lake Dam being built at Moran. Martha rode with him as he hauled dynamite to the construction site from the town of Jackson, following a newly made road on the west side of the Snake River.

That same year they homesteaded 160 acres on Mormon Row north of James May's original filing and east of land owned by Henrie May. They had little money and couldn't afford a home, so the Rinikers lived in cabins owned by Albert Gunther and C.L. Starrett as they started the tedious task of proving up on their homestead.

Within a couple of years they built a cabin for their growing family. The first born was Gordon, a year after their marriage. He was followed by Pauline, Rowena, Elaine, Dale, and Lois. Those children spent many a day with the May children and grandchildren playing cops and robbers in the hayloft of the big barn built by Robert I. May.

Like the other Mormon Row homesteaders, the Rinikers raised oats and barley, along with hay for their horses and the few cattle they had. When there was talk of building a cheese factory in Jackson, the family invested in some milk cows with the intention of selling products to the new factory.

Like so many promised operations, the cheese factory didn't get the support it needed because proponents couldn't find enough local farmers willing to milk cows to supply the necessary raw milk for cheese. The cheese factory never got beyond the promise stage which forced George and Martha to ship their cream to Nampa, Idaho. They sent it over Teton Pass to Victor, Idaho, on the stage, then it was loaded on the train for delivery in Nampa.

Undaunted by the difficulties of milking cows and shipping cream to Idaho, George and Rudy Harold then decided wool might be a marketable product. The two were the first ranchers to bring sheep to the east side of the Snake River. Some sheep ranching was underway on the west side of the river and George's brother-in-law, Nate Davis, had a small flock on his ranch.

The classic dispute between sheep and cattle ranchers extended to the valley. As early as 1901, cattlemen decreed there should and could be no sheep in Jackson Hole. In fact that year a flock was destroyed in an attack by raiders on Mosquito Creek.

So when George and Rudy decided they'd try raising sheep, they had historical disputes in their minds and fresh warnings ringing in their ears. They were told cattlemen would shoot any unwelcome woolies. The two remained undaunted. They picked up their flocks in Victor, Idaho, and herded them to Jackson Hole. As they headed over the Wilson Bridge, enroute to their ranches, both Rudy and George were armed in anticipation of a potentially deadly confrontation. It never materialized.

George and Rudy started with small flocks of perhaps a hundred sheep. Ironically, cattlemen who first resisted importation of sheep into Jackson Hole also later owned flocks of their own. Some other Mormon Row ranchers eventually had sheep which provided a fine cash crop in the form of mutton and wool.

George had one of his best lambing seasons in 1927 when most of his ewes had twins giving him a two hundred percent lamb crop. Unfortunately for him, that May Mother Nature dealt a busted flush when a natural disaster struck the valley.

George's older brother, John, moved to Jackson Hole from Butte, Montana, where he worked as a barber. Many of his customers were miners from Butte's numerous copper mines, but John gave up that profession because of what is called "Barber's Consumption." He was extremely allergic to dandruff, which caused him to have lung problems. John then went into the dairy business, which he continued until his younger brother George came to visit from Wyoming.

John joined George at Grovont where he homesteaded and built a frame house with a buck and pole fence. John loved horses and ran harness races on the tracks in Butte. After settling in Wyoming, he had a dandy little mare which he often hitched to his sulky to demonstrate harness racing at such local functions as the Fourth of July celebration in Jackson.

A group of early day Jackson Hole residents pauses before the fireplace in their crude cabin. (Photo Credit: Teton County Historical Center)

Like other young bachelors living in Jackson Hole, John found the loneliness of long winters almost unbearable, so he subscribed to a "Heart and Hand Club." John corresponded for a time with a lady subscriber to the club and things got to the marrying stage. John was ready to go and bring back to his homestead his chosen wife, a lady named Ethel, when friend and neighbor Hannes Harthoorn asked him to see if, by chance, Ethel knew a single woman who would also be interested in marriage.

Sure enough Ethel had a friend from England who jumped at the chance to meet an eligible bachelor. Margaret Crook accompanied John and Ethel Riniker back to Grovont from Ogden, Utah, and it wasn't long before Hannes had a new bride ensconced in his little log cabin.

Women were scarce in Jackson Hole and two other homesteaders on Mormon Row, Andy Cindle and Dick Van DeBrock, also turned to a Heart and Hand Club in Chicago for companionship. At almost the same time that Harthoorn and Riniker imported their wives from Utah, Cindle and Van DeBrock met their mail order brides in Victor, Idaho, to bring them to Jackson Hole.

Although the women may have helped relieve the tedium of bachelor living, Van DeBrock and Cindle found their mates didn't take to the hard work and isolation. In only a few short years the women convinced the men to sell their land and go with the girls back to Chicago.

Like other men determined to make a better life in America, Harthoorn had a zest for work. He plowed sod and

Binding grain west of the Hannes Harthoorn place with Henrie May on the binder and Clifton May driving the tractor. (Photo Credit: Clark and Veda Moulton Collection)

sage all day with four head of draft horses and a sixteen inch sulky plow. Then, after finishing evening chores and eating his supper, he would go back to the field and pile brush. As twilight spread its blush over the land he lit the sage, which popped and crackled and spiced the air with a pungent smell far into the evening.

Lester May, a grandson of James I. May, recalled one incident when several little boys in the neighborhood decided to pull a prank on Harthoorn. They went tick-tacking. A tick tack was made with a wooden spool that had notches cut all around the flanges. The boys wound a long string around the spool and ran a pencil through the center to serve as an axle. One boy held the device against the windowpane, then grabbed the string and ran as quickly as he could. The resulting noise alarmed any unsuspecting inhabitant of the house.

Lester May recalled the tick-tacking of Harthoorn this way:

Snow drifts were six or eight feet deep at the south side of Hannes' house and we slid down and proceeded to give Hannes the scare of his life. What we forgot was the impossibility of a little boy scrambling up the drift. No doubt the noise of the tick tack must have startled Hannes, but to this day I haven't been able to figure how he could have grabbed his shotgun and opened the door so quickly. We were scrambling trying to get up the drift when the shot rang out and we knew we were about to die.

The light from the window revealed us and Hannes hollered for us to surrender and come into the cabin. We knew he would at least give us the whipping of our lives. He told us to sit down and wait our fate. Then he opened a trap door into an underground cellar and disappeared down a ladder. Now we wondered if we should bolt for the door and escape, but we were too petrified to move.

Soon Hannes reappeared up through the floor with two hands full of bright red apples. Now things started looking up as apples were a rare treat at any time of the year. When each small miscreant had an apple Hannes reached up on a closet and brought down an accordion and began to play and sing. I've never heard more beautiful music in my life. Especially just after thinking I was facing certain death.

John Moulton, one of three brothers to settle on Mormon Row spent his last years living in Jackson. This photo was taken when he was 101. He died in 1990 at age 103. (Photo Credit: Olie Riniker)

Though some of the Mormon Row men imported their wives, John Moulton had no need to resort to a "Lonely Hearts" club for a mate. When his brother Alma's wife Lucile was due to give birth to one of her children her sister, Bartha Blanchard, came over from Idaho to help.

Lester May said:

> She, being the astute business woman she was, saw great potential in this young bachelor and forthwith set her cap for him. If all the bachelors of the area had used the same judgment this handsome homesteader used they would have solved their labor, mate and business manager needs in one fell swoop.

The couple started life together in John's small homestead cabin. Soon four children completed the family, Hilma, Frances, Boyd, and Reed.

John was good with his horses, but early during the Great Depression Bartha could see the need for a local supply for dairy products and the services that went with the early rise of the tourist industry in Jackson Hole and Yellowstone National Park. The family went into the dairy business, supplying and running a milk route to most of the dude ranches in the area. The enterprise supplemented the family's cattle operation as deliveries went to the business establishments and the campgrounds in Yellowstone.

John Moulton's barn in 1993. (Photo Credit: Candy Moulton)

Bartha also had about sixty chickens. She bartered for food and other necessities with the eggs the hens laid. She also taught the children with them. One winter the youngsters got a dozen eggs if they learned their multiplication tables up to nine. The eggs could be taken to Kelly and sold. That was spending money, a rare commodity for the children, and incentive to learn math. Hilma bought a dog with her money.

When he arrived at Mormon Row in 1907, John Moulton had a coal oil lamp. He got his first gas lamp in 1924, six years before he had a car and a decade before he had a telephone installed in his home. Electricity became a reality even more decades later.

Thomas Perry was a carpenter by trade, having settled on Mormon Row along with the Moultons. He had a quarter section north of Hannes Harthoorn and across the lane from Joe Eggleston. He gave an acre in the southwest corner of his land to the church, which he also built. No doubt the other members contributed some labor, but Perry was the contractor.

The well-digging Joe Pfeiffer spent his childhood in Wheeling, West Virginia, where he was born in 1878, but he left his home to see the Bowery and the Barbary Coast. He caught a train headed for Jersey City, and eventually met a young actor who gave wise advice, saving Pfeiffer from a possible mugging. Pfeiffer roamed the country for a dozen years, finally landing in Butte, Montana, where he worked in a mine before hopping a stage for Idaho and eventually the trip to Jackson Hole. In Idaho he heard stories about the outlaws in Wyoming. He said:

> We'd listen to the talk about outlaws' hideouts. The damn fools were crazy. You couldn't live in these mountains, keep a horse or feed. An outlaw would have known better. An outlaw wouldn't come in country like this.

The first rows of the Chambers barn didn't remain as straight as Andy Chambers wanted them so he sought help from his friend and neighbor, Alma Moulton. The barn and homestead stood abandoned on Mormon Row in 1993, having stood the test of time, but beginning to show neglect from disuse. (Photo Credit: Candy Moulton)

In 1912 Andy Chambers acquired the last homestead unit on Mormon Row. He borrowed the money to buy a team and then started the hard, back-breaking labor of clearing and cultivating the land. When he started his log barn, Andy found the task daunting. He put up the first four rows of fresh logs and noticed they were tipped. He went to Alma Moulton for advice on how to keep the walls straight. Moulton showed Chambers his method for building solid, straight walls. The difference in the men's styles of log work is still apparent at the abandoned homestead.

In February of 1918, Andy hitched his sleigh and took a young school teacher, Ida B. Kneedy, out of Jackson Hole over

Teton Pass to Driggs, Idaho, to make her his bride. The young couple then returned to the ranch, but wedded bliss was not to be. Uncle Sam sent greetings and Andy was off to fight in World War I. Ida remained behind to run the homestead. Andy returned from war to find things well in hand on the home-front. He and Ida soon started a family that included Vera, Roy, Reese, Cora, Inez, Glen, and Anita.

Ida shared the hard work even after Andy returned to the homestead. On one occasion they each drove a team and wagon full of grain to Yellowstone where they sold it for the unheard of high sum of five dollars per sack. From 1923 until 1935 Ida ran the Grovont Post Office out of her home while Andy had the mail route in the valley.

The post office pay was minimal. All the post mistress received was the money taken in from the sale of stamps. Many days went by when there was no income at all, but the land always provided and during the Depression, when so many men were out of work, Andy Chambers produced enough from his acreage to care for five families.

Ida Chambers in 1987. She lost her parents in the Kelly Flood of 1927 and raised a stalwart family that remained actively working the Grovont area land until the 1980s.
(Photo Credit: Olie Riniker)

Crossing Teton Pass in deep snow.
(Photo Credit: Teton County Historical Center)

The Mountain Slid

Give it a wet enough year and all that rocky strata will just slide right down on that gumbo like a beaver's slickery slide.

—Billy Bierers, Gros Ventre homesteader

Gros Ventre Indians felt the ground constantly shifting beneath their moccasin-covered feet as they moved up the river canyon that bears their name. They listened to a dull rumbling at night when they lay in their robes upon the ground.

With their heads on the red soil they felt the ground tremble. It sounded like a stampede of buffalo and the Indians believed the ground along Sheep Mountain and the Gros Ventre would quiver when the Indians who roamed in an underground valley were hunting the buffalo that lived in the earth's bowels. It was a beautiful canyon, but the native

Americans didn't feel comfortable and they seldom stayed long on the river.

The Gros Ventre gave their name to a large mountain range at the eastern edge of Jackson Hole and the clear river that slashed down the canyon. Though trappers no doubt found the river a prime source of beaver and as good a place as any other to spend the winters, no one lived permanently high up along the river until homesteaders claimed land.

Billy Bierers settled in 1895 on the west side of the river near Sheep Mountain where he built a little cabin and worked his land. As he went about his chores, Bierers observed the mountains around him. He saw the deer and elk that made their homes there, he viewed beaver in the creeks and the river, and he watched Sheep Mountain.

"Anywhere on that slope, if I lay my ear to the ground, I can heard water tricklin' and runnin' underneath. It's running between strata and some day, if we have a wet enough spring, that whole mountain is gonna let loose and slide," Bierers said.

The mountain is a heavy rocky strata overlaying bentonitic clays. Those clays, when exposed on the surface, turn into gumbo which cakes on a person's boots when it rains and sticks like cement when it dries. Bierers wasn't a geologist, but he knew from watching the area that when it got wet enough the rock would slide down into the river canyon. An earth

Billy Bierers predicted the Gros Ventre Slide, saying he could hear water running under the ground in that area and some day it would come down "like a beaver's slickery slide." Bierers sold his homestead to Guil Huff and wasn't around when the mountain fell. (Photo Credit: Teton County Historical Center)

tremor would rock the area just when the ground was the wettest, he predicted.

> Yes, I have noticed and I cannot see where the water can be going unless it is following the formation between two different stratifications and coming to the surface at some other water-level point. If not, this mountainside would be a mushy, woozy boil. However it may be, there is a wet line running between stratas and the time will come when the entire mountain will slip down into the canyon below. For instance, some of these times these earthquake tremors that are coming so often are going to hit at about the right time when the mountain is the wooziest, and down she'll come.

The evidence was clear. Minor slides occurred all along the river at various times. A slow slide ran in 1911 and 1912 damming the river above Bierers place. In that geologic event the earth moved gradually, a bit at a time until it blocked the river and formed a long lake in the canyon valley.

"Give it a wet enough year and all that rocky strata will just slide right down on that gumbo like a beaver's slickery slide," Bierers predicted.

The homesteader sold his land in 1920 to Guil Huff, and then Bierers left Jackson Hole to live with a daughter in the East. Having the Bierers homestead pleased the Huffs. Its location on the Gros Ventre was in an area where plenty of meadow grasses provided feed for their cattle in the winter. Those same cows could be pushed up onto forest lands to graze during the summer.

Guil and Violet Huff put all their savings and work into the ranch and home. They built a lovely log house on the bench overlooking the river. A cabinet maker by trade, Huff used his skills to make his home comfortable. The family was settled with five-year-old daughter Dorothy when one spring day their world literally was torn asunder.

The winter of 1925 had been one of unusually heavy snows that continued to fall well into May. Nearly continual rains followed the wet spring snow, saturating the ground.

On the afternoon of June 23, 1925, Guil Huff hitched four

head of horses to the plow and worked in his lower field. Through the day he heard boulders rolling and saw some dust spirals up on Sheep Mountain. He finally decided to quit tilling early to ride to check on the cows, and to see what was causing the dust and the noise.

Huff returned his work teams to the main buildings, saddled his horse, and started up the slope to investigate the disturbance on the mountain. He was out of the meadow gate and on the hillside above the river when the occasional thump of a boulder turned into a steady purr. When Huff looked up, a brown mist rose from a stand of lodgepole pine, swirling and drifting in the sun's rays. As he listened to the hum and watched the dust, he saw the trees begin to move, twisting, leaning, tossing, and then rushing toward him. The sound became a roar and the earth started to move.

Huff wheeled his horse, but had no need to spur the animal, which took off down the trail toward home and safety.

An abandoned sled on Mormon Row points to the Gros Ventre Slide scar on Sheep Mountain. (Photo Credit: Candy Moulton)

Cowboys Forney Cole, Leonard Peterson, and Boyd Charter were across the river, high up on the canyon slope. Cole had moved some strays out of Huff's meadow. Peterson was bringing some cattle along the two-rut road and Charter had just caught up with them.

The men were catching up on news when they heard rocks rolling and looked up at a roaring sound to see strange dust spirals and then a cloud of dirt. They watched as the mountainside seemed to be moving and spreading out. The cowboys used their spurs and legs to grip their increasingly excited horses as they watched the slide head for Huff's ranch.

Charter hesitated only seconds before spurring his horse up the river canyon toward the Horsetail Ranger Station. While Charter tore along the road, the other two cowboys watched in horror as Guil Huff engaged in a race for his life with a mass of granite, trees, and boulders. He was trying to outrun a mountain.

U

Bob Seaton was on a steep slope above Turpin Creek and did not see the slide. He heard it. The roar of the mountain and the shaking of the earth scared Seaton and his horse so badly they raced down the road toward Kelly without stopping to see what was causing the valley to race and growl.

U

Dust from Sheep Mountain attracted Mormon Row homesteader Ned Budge's gaze as he rode up Turpin Creek searching for horses that June day. He heard a loud hissing sound that quickly turned into a roar. Ned saw the top of the slide start moving and slipping down the hill before he raced for home, deciding he could hunt horses another time.

U

Violet and Dorothy Huff were home when the mountain's movement started. Violet looked out the window and saw the top of the slide. She recalled:

> Trees started moving and tipping. Dust rose above them. I wondered for a minute then I realized what it was. I called Dorothy, who was playing nearby. "Come look out the window, a slide is running up on the mountain." She didn't stop playing and I could not see the lower part of it so I didn't know how close it was coming.

Violet also didn't know the slide put her husband in mortal danger.

Guil reached the meadow fence just as the massive jumble of rocks and trees rushed past him, thundering into the riverbed. He had won the first leg of his desperate race.

As Peterson and Cole raced their horses toward the Huff

place to lend aid, Charter spurred his horse toward the ranger station. Huff watched over his shoulder as the vast mass of mountain debris hit the near perpendicular wall of the north side of the narrow valley. It split. The upstream part of the mass, under tremendous pressure, forced its way up the canyon, following Huff who continued in his flight from the moving mountain. Boulders flew past him as did trees that seemed to be outrunning the horse. Huff was nearly to his front yard before he was clearly out of danger.

∪

Supper was ready, but they didn't eat.

The family, assisted by Peterson and Cole, immediately started loading its possessions into a wagon. They didn't know if other slides would race during the upcoming night, but they could easily see the dammed river and the rising water.

∪

Forest Ranger C.E. Dibble was a stranger to the Gros Ventre country. He moved to Horsetail Ranger Station with his wife, Alberta, and daughter from the Weiser National Forest in western Idaho only one week before Sheep Mountain started its momentous movement.

At about 4:20 p.m. on June 23, 1925, he heard a rumbling, grating noise. The ranger was unsure what the noise signified and went about his work until a few minutes later when a long-legged young cowboy thundered into the yard. Cowboy Boyd Charter, rushed to tell Dibble about the avalanche of rocks and trees and mud that he had watched slide into the river.

The young puncher, in a tumble of words laced with profanity because of his excitement, told how the mountain face simply broke away. He apologized to Dibble for his epithets, but they spewed from his mouth unbidden as he told a frightening tale.

A block of earth estimated to be a mile and a half long and a mile wide had fallen. In places the part that tore away was hundreds of feet deep as the whole section let go its grip on the mountain and gravity took it crashing into the canyon. It took only two or three minutes for the slide to rush down.

The ranger heard the eyewitness account from the young cowboy, then he got his Model T and the two rushed up the road toward the Huff ranch.

All that night Dibble, the three cowboys, and the Huffs worked. They hauled the family's possessions from their house, suddenly perilously close to the fast-rising, newly-formed lake, to the ranger station located upstream and on higher ground. As the Huffs worked, a similar evacuation took place at the William Card ranch located near Huffs and also in danger of flooding.

Rancher Guil Huff stands atop a building to survey the havoc wrought by the Gros Ventre Slide in 1925. Huff's ranch soon lay under Slide Lake, which was formed when the natural disaster dammed the Gros Ventre River. (Photo Credit: Teton County Historical Center)

While the men and women loaded and hauled goods from the homes to the ranger station, small slides continued to run down the mountain. Each time a boulder gave way and the noise pitched to a whine, young Boyd Charter jumped and prepared for a quick getaway muttering, "I'll be glad when this job is done."

Just before dawn the tense work finally ended as the Huffs fell into an exhausted sleep on a mattress on the floor of the ranger station office cabin.

As the sun rose over the newly-scarred Sheep Mountain, Guil, Violet, and Dorothy Huff returned to their home to find it already about eighteen inches under the water of the lake naturally christened Slide Lake. The water body formed earlier from a similar rock movement soon was Upper Slide Lake.

Trees laced the dam. They were criss-cross, horizontal, vertical, and leaning at every conceivable angle. One of the first to write about the great landslide was William O. Owen. He was familiar with the area having surveyed it for the government in 1892–93. In making that survey he noticed that the soil is "naturally disposed to slides and is generally treacherous where the slopes become at all steep."

In a manuscript written in September of 1925, Owen wrote:

> Some of the great spruces and firs are still standing erect and virile, as vigorous and as firmly planted as before the slide occurred, although many of them are a mile and a half from the spot on Sheep Mountain where their tiny sprouts first shot through the soil to kiss the sun, some hundreds of years ago!
>
> It is of interest to note that most all of the springs on the south side of the river, in the near vicinity of the slide, instantly ceased flowing, and have shown no sign of life since.

Soon after the slide raced, a stream of people started up the Gros Ventre to view the destruction. Among the first to arrive were Forest Supervisor A.C. McCain, Ranger Felix Buckenroth, Dick Winger, Donald Hough, and Guil Huff's brother, Dr. Charles W. Huff of Jackson.

They drove to the downstream edge of the slide, then climbed the mountain on the canyon's north face to get to Guil Huff's home. When they left, Guil, Violet, and Dorothy accompanied them. Their homestead along the Gros Ventre had been ripped from them in mere minutes. Their ranch meadow land was under water and their house would soon float onto the lake, but they had saved most of their personal possessions and their lives.

Guil wouldn't wait for a new road to be built to the ranger's station to retrieve his belongings. He and Henry Francis used a pack string to haul their possessions over the mountain and away from the lake that buried their dreams.

Ranger Dibble and his family remained at the Horsetail Station through the end of June. The water in Slide Lake rose steadily and they planned to leave the first of July. By the time the stars twinkled on June 29, water lapped near the ranger station. Dibble said they would leave the next day.

It rained hard all afternoon and into the night. The downpour thoroughly soaked the mountain at the other side of the lake and the family began to fear another slide. Their belongings packed, the Dibbles crawled into their beds. About midnight a roar awakened them. Alberta jumped from her bed, ran to the door, peered out into the black night, and yelled, "It is coming."

Dibble scooped up his six-year-old daughter and the family fled out the back door. Wearing only their night clothes, they raced up the hill going through a barbed wire fence that pierced and tore their garments and their flesh. They ran until the roar quieted. Cautiously they returned to their home where they donned dry clothes. Then taking their Model T, they drove to a high spot and pitched a tent in which they spent the balance of the night.

The nighttime roar they feared didn't come from another slide. When the sun pinkened the eastern sky, the Dibbles saw that the mountain had settled, making large terraces. The movement caused water to wash up against the foundation of the ranger station. That day the ranger and his family gathered their belongings and left Horsetail Ranger Station. Three days later it floated away on the lake.

Down in the valley at Grovont the settlers of Mormon Row were unaware of the devastation wrought by nature until the morning after the first slide. From their homes and the lane, the homesteaders could look at the mountain and see the huge fan-shaped scar.

Because of the heavy rain and resulting muddy road conditions, it was a few days before people could easily get to the area. The John Moulton family and some relatives visiting from Idaho hitched a team to their spring wagon for the trip up to the scene of destruction. They marveled at the scar on the earth, and gaped at the trees tipped and tilting or completely overturned, their bare roots pointing toward the sun. Their faces showed shock as they saw the ranches being covered with water. The homesteaders knew what work went into carving a homestead and that years of drudgery had been quickly eliminated by a force of nature.

The Moultons turned their wagon back down the canyon toward their homestead, thankful that the destruction had taken no lives and that it hadn't touched their own land. But, nature hadn't run its course along the Gros Ventre yet; a further calamity was building up in the clear, blue waters of Slide Lake.

A Wall of
Water

A serpent of huge size crawling down the valley.
—County School Superintendent Martha
Marean's description of the Kelly flood

Kelly, located midway between Grovont and Slide Lake at the mouth of the Gros Ventre Canyon, was an up-and-coming place in 1925 when Sheep Mountain crashed into the canyon.

Fearing a further landslide would break the massive dam that had been naturally constructed during the June earth movement, Kelly residents kept an ear tuned and an eye turned toward the river. They routinely left their homes at night and headed for high ground, but the expected break didn't occur, and geologic experts from throughout the country assured citizens that the dam would hold, so they finally reduced their vigilance.

The Gros Ventre Slide path was about a quarter of a mile wide. The top was at an elevation of 9,025 feet and the mountain slid vertically 2,225 feet to dump itself in the river bed that had an elevation of 6,800 feet. A straight line from the upper line of the slide's path to the old river bed measured nearly two miles.

When it settled, the mountain formed a dam with a crown width of one thousand feet. The lower face dropped at a comparatively steep grade for about sixty feet in elevation and then spread out about a half-mile downstream.

The dam rose to a height of about 180 feet above the natural streambed and created a lake a half mile wide and four miles long. It impounded about sixty-five thousand acre feet of water. The dam itself was of sandstone, limestone, and shale varying in size from fine sand to boulders and chunks as large as houses. The rocks intermingled with trees and other vegetation to the point that soon after the slide Wyoming State Engineer Frank C. Emerson estimated that decomposed material made up twenty-five to thirty percent of the dam's mass.

For a two-week period immediately after the slide, the natural check effectively sealed flows in the river halting the ten thousand acre-feet of water needed by downstream homesteaders to irrigate crops. Fortunately for them continued heavy rains covered fields naturally.

State Engineer Emerson and a host of other experts declared the dam substantial and not likely to be affected by rising waters. The people living downstream need not worry, they were told. Eventually the waters in the lake would rise and likely flow over the lower, less stable south end of the dam in an area that was a natural spillway.

Before long the water did start to trickle through the south end of the dam and the Gros Ventre began flowing again, taking water to Kelly and the homesteaders in Jackson Hole.

The people of Kelly put aside their fears that the earth would breach. Ranger C.E. Dibble, who remained in the region following the slide of 1925, first noticed something wrong with the river on a clear, sunny day two years later.

Slide Lake lapped at its banks and the top of the two-year-old natural dam on May 17, 1927. Another heavy-snow winter and wet spring swelled the Gros Ventre and its tributaries so they ran high—roaring and pouring into the already-full lake.

Kelly residents, a few miles downstream from Slide Lake didn't worry that spring. After all, the dam had held for two years; they figured by now all the material had settled and compacted. Besides, eminent engineers had pronounced it safe. A nightmare in broad daylight was about to occur.

On the morning of May 18, 1927, the Gros Ventre was bank-full. C. E. Dibble and others were at the Kelly bridge working to keep logs and driftwood from lodging against it. The men noticed an unusual amount of debris in the river that morning, but they paid little attention as they worked to keep the bridge free. Then Dibble saw spiraling in the channel something that chilled him. Heading down the turbulent Gros Ventre was a hayrack he had seen often—floating in the middle of Slide Lake.

Dibble and another man jumped into the ranger's Model T and headed upriver. About three and a half miles above Kelly they met a wall of water. Turning the car they careened back toward town, stopping to cut fence wires and allow stock to escape from pastures and the path of the flood that threatened Jackson Hole.

Flood waters surged under the Kelly bridge as a flood swept down the Gros Ventre River in 1927, destroying the small town of Kelly. (Photo Credit: Teton County Historical Center)

The water toppled a log house, as if it were a child's toy. Dibble stopped at one ranch long enough to warn the occupants and have them make telephone calls to others living along the river. Then he raced toward Kelly, the Model T going as fast as it could and Dibble spurring the seat in an effort to get more speed out of the vehicle.

In Kelly he spread the news of the water wall, which was even then perilously close to the community. People had only about fifteen minutes to get what they could quickly grab. Then they headed for high ground.

As the rampant stream cascaded its way toward town, fourteen school children raced for their homes and residents worked feverishly to save their belongings. Donald Kent, a student at the Kelly school that day, said, "My father showed up at the school and he told me to come on get out of there, get our three saddle horses, and get to higher ground up north. The other children got out not too long after that, but the bridge was floating when I rode across it."

All residents along the Gros Ventre and in Kelly had harrowing experiences during the next few hours as the freshet tore through the area.

$$\cup$$

For weeks after the creation of Slide Lake, Anna Kneedy and her son Joe, left their home along the river every evening to sleep on higher ground. H. M. Kneedy ridiculed their fears until eventually the woman and boy decided they would stay in their home near Kelly at night.

When Ranger Dibble rushed to the Kneedy grist mill along the river to tell them a wall of water was fast approaching, Kneedy refused to believe the tale. Dibble made two attempts to get the family to understand it must evacuate the area immediately. Kneedy scorned the ranger saying he must be badly scared or crazy.

Joe Kneedy, then age ten, was taken to safety twice, and each time he returned to his home. When asked to leave a third time he said he was going to get his mother, but the river caught him and his family first. All drowned in the rampaging Gros Ventre.

Mr. and Mrs. Frank Almy were in their car when the force

of the water hit it. The car, which had no top, overturned and the wild water grabbed the elderly couple. The current sucked Mrs. Almy under the dark, churning waters time and again as floodwaters poured down the valley. She rolled and bumped along in the surge for almost a mile before she finally dragged herself partway to safety. As she lay exhausted in the roiling water, Mrs. Almy heard someone call to her.

A man named Shorty hauled a load of wheat to Kelly that day and, perhaps frozen with fear, did nothing to save himself when the water approached. The river dragged his team under and one horse broke loose to save itself. The other drowned. The force of the current hurled Shorty from the wagon into the water. He managed to get out of the cauldron in the same place Mrs. Almy broke free. He directed her to safety and helped pull her to shore even though he was so cold his body was numb. Frank Almy also survived, though the tale of how he escaped the angry water isn't documented.

Before the waters receded, the flood claimed six lives. One entire family died in the flood: H.M. Kneedy, his wife Anna, and stepson Joe. Other victims were Maud Smith, her sister May Lovejoy, and Clint Stevens.

Grovont homesteaders weren't unaware of the tragedy at Kelly as they had been upon the formation of Slide Lake. They heard the roar of the river and stood on their porches watching the thirty to fifty foot high wall of water as it destroyed Kelly. They were the first to get to the scene of destruction and offer aid. For many weeks afterward—when they turned their church into a morgue—they were involved in the cataclysmic event.

The stories of heroic escapes, rescues, and unfortunate blunders that lead to death etched themselves deeply in the minds and hearts of Grovont homesteaders. Through the years they continued to tell the stories of escapes and near escapes, of death that came to their peaceful valley.

Notified of the impending flood, sisters May Lovejoy and Maud Smith quickly harnessed their team and threw what household valuables they could into the wagon before they saw the water approaching. The women jumped into the buckboard and careened away from their home in a desperate attempt to outrun the flood.

A rancher saw their flight as the women turned the wagon at a right angle to the fast-approaching on-rush of water. The horses strained and pulled with one sister holding the lines and driving and the other whipping the animals in a vain effort to outrun the flood. As they ran, the current caught the wagon and tossed the women into the surge. Both died. Neighbors found Maud Smith's body a half mile downstream. Searchers never recovered that of her sister.

The rancher watching the plight of the women was hoping they would outrun the raging waters, and had they turned and run at an angle away from the flow, rather than at a straight line in front of the tide, perhaps there would be a different ending to their story.

Max Edick, Mike Meeks, Floyd True, and Jack Moore saved themselves by clinging to trees. Edick and a hired hand were trying to save some pigs and chickens when the flood bore down on them. The two climbed to the roof of the chicken house and stayed there until a hayrack floated by. The hired hand jumped on the hayrack; his body was wedged in a tree four miles downstream.

Edick remained on the chicken house which soon floated into the current. As the small shed went past a ten-inch diameter spruce tree, Edick grabbed the branches and pulled himself above the roiling waters. He remained in the tree until rescue arrived in the form of Mormon Row resident Allen Budge who was riding a pretty good swimming horse.

Jack Moore warned Mike Meeks and Floyd True of the flood, but when Moore reached Meeks' cabin along the Gros Ventre the three realized their situation was grim. Neither Mike nor Floyd had a horse, but the three decided to head down an old wagon road. Mike rode the horse with Floyd hanging on to the pony's tail and Jack tied to a rope from the saddle. The three soon knew they couldn't outpace the freshet so they also hastened up a tree. Legend has it that all three shinnied up the same tree where they remained until the flow receded. The horse ran free, but apparently became caught in the surging waters. It disappeared.

Lester May was a boy when the flood hit, but in 1993 he

The Kelly flood waters spread more than a mile wide, wiped out the town of Kelly, and damaged ranches, bridges, and the town of Wilson. (Photo Credit: Teton County Historical Center)

clearly remembered George Riniker riding to the May house hollering, "We're having a flood, we're having a flood." May joined other Grovont homesteaders at the river's edge, riding the shoreline looking for survivors. The following day the Mormon Row men and others from Jackson Hole started the grim task of looking for bodies.

Clark Moulton and Veda May (Moulton), who were just teenagers, watched from their homes and the Mormon Row LDS church steps, staring in awe at the waves of black water carrying houses and haystacks down a mile-wide channel.

The flood left well over one hundred people homeless; many lost everything except the clothes on their backs as the waters rushed through the valley. It destroyed homes at the mouth of the Gros Ventre and at Kelly, then surged downstream to do further damage below Menor's Ferry and in Wilson where hundreds of cattle died and the water stood six feet deep.

In Kelly after the water dropped, just the church, parsonage, schoolhouse, and Hilmar Bark building remained.

Everything else was stripped bare; there were no trees or grass and only a heap of boulders and cobblestones marked the site.

There are two theories about what caused the tragedy. The first pertains to the south side of the 1925 slide area that filled last. Loose materials, mainly yellow clay and sandstone, composed that portion of the dam. Some say the natural seepage water so saturated this material that the high water just naturally pushed the great mass of it out, bodily letting the flood run.

The other explanation is that a slide which came in from the north, perhaps caused by an earth tremor, sent a wave of water over the Slide Lake Dam that carried away enough of the soft material on the south side to start the water over the dam and then the water rapidly washed through the loose earth.

Whatever the cause, the devastated strip of land left behind was a narrow swath only about three miles wide, but the aftermath of the disaster reached farther. It was spring time, that time of year when crops are planted and must be irrigated. The rushing waters filled ditches with boulders, dirt, and debris,

Left: After the 1927 flood that ripped through Kelly, few buildings remained. One that still stood was this building, the Hilmar Bark House, that later became the Kelly post office. Right: The Episcopal Church in Kelly also survived the flood of 1927 and later it, too, served as the town's post office. (Photo Credit: Teton County Historical Center)

The Kelly flood of 1927 caused widespread devastation through Jackson Hole. (Photo Credit: Teton County Historical Center)

ruined headgates used to divert water from the river to cropland, and damaged other land by covering it with rocks and rubbish.

County School Superintendent Martha Marean described the flood as, "A serpent of huge size crawling down the valley. As the main current hit an obstacle it swerved to the opposite shore, its venomous children crawling down the irrigation ditches."

As the water raced and roared, George Riniker's flock of sheep split. Most of the older ewes and rams made it to higher ground, but many of the lambs ran the wrong direction and the flood waters grabbed them. His two hundred percent lamb crop died in the roiling water.

Martha Davis Riniker recalled the flood:

We was right on the Gros Ventre River, you know. We knew it was raising but we didn't know it was a flood. We got notice that it was raising—the next door neighbors had the word, they got to them. But the neighbor that gave us the warning went on top of his barn to undo his horses to let them out and it just washed out from under him. The only way he saved himself, he went under the big trees and he grabbed a limb and saved his life.

When you see the water coming at you as high as the mountains—I thought it was the mountains! It had trees and horses with harnesses on, coming right at us when we run our team out. We had to get up next to the [Blacktail] butte.

In addition to losing the major portion of their lamb crop that soggy spring day when the dam broke, the Rinikers lost their barn and chicken coop, along with all their chickens and pigs, and much of the machinery stored in the machine shed. Their house survived, but was filled with mud.

They were forced to return to the Mormon Row cabin, which had not been lived in for some time. They fixed it enough to move in during the time they were cleaning and repairing the Gros Ventre ranch. They built a makeshift barn from the scraps of lumber that floated their way during the

Flood waters raced over Teton Valley Ranch in 1927. (Photo Credit: Teton County Historical Center)

flood, using boards and hay for a temporary roof. Their circumstances were bad, but not really any worse than those of many other residents along the Gros Ventre after that flood ripped down the valley.

As the extent of the tragedy became known, Mormon Row residents became closely involved. They set up an emergency morgue in the church. Men of the community nailed together rude coffins and weeping women ironically packed buckets of water from the ditch to clean those who had perished. They grieved as they dressed and laid out their dead friends and relatives.

The Red Cross quickly joined the rescue and rebuilding effort, establishing a headquarters at the James I. May house on the south end of the lane. There Mrs. VanLevin, Mae Kafferlin and Hadden May distributed, and kept track of, emergency supplies.

Hundreds of cows died in the 1927 Kelly Flood near Wilson as the Gros Ventre and Snake Rivers raged out of their channels. This view of the flood in Wilson shows the Mike Yokel home in the foreground, now site of the Stagecoach Bar. (Photo Credit: Teton County Historical Center)

Eighteen families took aid including those of both George and John Riniker. John's deliveries ranged from a child's union suit and sweater to rag rugs, stockings, coats, and pants. For food he received bacon, sugar, salt, flour, vegetables, eggs, and spices. John also accepted a percolator and candles. Taking handouts wasn't something self-reliant people liked to do, but in this case they had to accept assistance.

The Mormon Row homesteaders were late in planting their crops that spring; they had been too busy helping less fortunate neighbors who lost their homes and loved ones in the flood. When they planted crops in early in June, the homesteaders knew they would be hard pressed to mature. Rocks and mud filled the irrigation ditches, temporarily ruining their use as water conveyances.

Some good came from the flood for the Grovont families, because state and federal aid poured in making it possible to rebuild the irrigation ditches, and finish those that had never been completed.

After the flood, the area was assured it could get water from the Gros Ventre to raise hay and oats. The settlers gave thanks for their fortune. Their appreciation became more profound when, shortly after the flood, a warm spring developed at the mouth of Gros Ventre canyon.

That natural spring provided running water for the Moultons and others homesteading along the north end of the row near Blacktail Butte. For more than twenty years the families had hauled river water, but a disaster brought a blessing. No longer did they have to trek regularly to the Gros Ventre to get water for gardens or livestock; now a small creek provided it naturally. Because the water was warm, it ran year around. Mormon Row residents called it the Miracle Spring.

Seasons of Time

A few years ago a fella drove in, figuring no one was living here. He starts picking up some old wheels and things and loading 'em in his car. I went out to give him a hand. We got it loaded up, and he drove off.
—Joe Pfeiffer, *American West*, 1965

Time marched on for the Grovont homesteaders as they turned their land from sagebrush to crops and marked the passage of the years with new buildings, new neighbors and children, or death and tragedy.

Life was a never ending struggle for survival, but there was inspiration too, as the Grovont homesteaders watched the seasons pass over the land and the Tetons they could see to the west. The homesteaders tilled their soil, harvested their crops, and enjoyed the bounty of the area as the years cycled. The play of the sunshine and weather changes marked the days.

When the fresh shoots of green poked through receding

snows and the songbirds returned to the high country, Grovont homesteaders knew winter was yielding its grip on the land and it was time to start anew.

The women cleaned their dirt-roofed cabins from top to bottom. They hauled out the rag rugs, which they had woven from worn strips of cloth during the long winters, to beat them and wash them. They took straw-filled bed ticks from the boards they rested on to air outdoors. Inside and outside they scrubbed, swept, and straightened the house. Then they turned to the business of planting.

Their menfolk plowed garden plots for peas, beans, potatoes, carrots, and other vegetables. The men prepared the spot willingly enough for they knew that the crops their wives tended would add variety to the table throughout the year, but they didn't spend much time around the house as spring came to the land.

Men had work of their own to do so they hitched teams and headed to the fields to prepare the soil for hay and the ninety-day oats that James I. May had brought with him. That strain grew and matured quickly so a harvest could be made in a country with an extremely short growing season. The men knew if they planted by mid-May they might be able to sneak through the last hard freeze of the year that could come in late June, and have the oats ready to reap by mid-August before the first fall frost nipped the air. Of course they knew and expected snow to fall almost every month of the year, but that wouldn't kill the crops if the mercury didn't dip too low.

As the grass started to grow, the neighbors on Mormon Row generally ran their cows on Antelope Flats until spring roundup when they moved over to Ditch Creek, Turpin Creek or Horse Tail Creek. During the gathering the homesteaders became cowboys as they herded all the stock together into one big group of from eight hundred to a thousand head. Then the work really started as the men and boys sorted the cattle to brand and dehorn the calves that had been born during the early spring.

In Wyoming there was never any question of which calf belonged to which owner since the young animal was branded with the same mark as the cow he nursed. The Mormon Row homesteaders ran their cattle under a variety of brands including the Bar Ox Hoof of T.A. Moulton, the Seven Lazy Three of James I. May, the Spear M of Henrie May, the Double D and the Bar Cross of Jim Budge, the L Quarter Circle K of Wallace Moulton, the Division Mark of Tom Murphy, the DYV of Dick Van DeBrock, the Lazy RV of George Riniker, the 6 Lazy Mill Iron of John Moulton, and the Walking R of Roy McBride.

Following roundup and branding, cows and calves roamed freely over the area that is now Grand Teton National Park. The

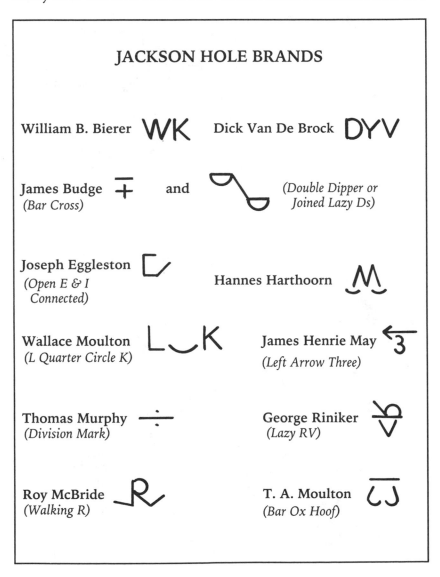

JACKSON HOLE BRANDS

William B. Bierer WK   **Dick Van De Brock** DYV

James Budge ┼ **and**   *(Double Dipper or Joined Lazy Ds)*
(Bar Cross)

Joseph Eggleston   **Hannes Harthoorn** M
(Open E & I Connected)

Wallace Moulton L⌣K   **James Henrie May**
(L Quarter Circle K)   *(Left Arrow Three)*

Thomas Murphy ÷   **George Riniker**
(Division Mark)   *(Lazy RV)*

Roy McBride R   **T. A. Moulton**
(Walking R)   *(Bar Ox Hoof)*

homesteaders didn't pay for the use of the grazing land until their cattle entered the forest preserve.

Beef sold for about seven cents per pound and the only markets were in Omaha and Chicago. That meant the homesteaders had to gather the animals they wanted to sell in the fall and trail them over Teton Pass to the Idaho railhead where they loaded onto the train for a four or five day trip to Nebraska or Illinois. Beef was about the only cash crop the settlers had, although some women sold butter, eggs, and cream.

The shortness of the mild seasons in Jackson Hole left the homesteaders with much to do and little time in which to get the work done. Summer was a frantic season as the men irrigated their hay and grain crops and then began the chore of stacking hay.

When James May first picked his piece of ground at Grovont he did so because the sagebrush was thick and tall indicating rich soil. He also had an eye for the logistics of raising crops since he knew it would be necessary to irrigate those same products in order to get any real harvest. As a result, one of the first things May did was to engineer ditches to divert water from the Gros Ventre River and transport it to his homestead. May marked the fields and dug ditches by hand or with a team of horses and fresno so water could be gotten to thirsty crops.

Della May and son LaVar, 1914. (Photo Credit: Clark and Veda Moulton Collection)

"To a farm kid such as I there was great satisfaction in building a high levee and watching the irrigation water . . . begin spreading out through the thirsty hay. The joyous sounds of the insects and birds as the water spread out through the meadows are among the most cherished of my childhood," Henrie May's son Lester said.

When the men and boys weren't busy with routine chores, they did general cleanup and improvements. As Lester May said:

Dad, as was true of most of the fathers of the time, could always find plenty for growing boys to do that did a very effective job of keeping boys out of mischief. One never ending chore we boys always had to do during, so called, slack time was haul manure. Keeping cattle and horses confined and fed in close quarters for long periods as we were forced to do in the long hard winters produced tons and tons of manure. This large accumulation of nature's choice fertilizer had to be removed each year by hard back-breaking methods. Much of this product was used to construct levees and dikes to control the irrigation water. Then the balance was for years hand-scattered on the meadows with teams and wagons and small boys with five-tined manure forks. Great was the rejoicing when Dad purchased the first "Gallaway" manure spreader. Now the team could at least unload the stuff even tho it still had to be loaded.

There were other uses for manure as well. The pioneers on Mormon Row, like others before them and no doubt others of their era in different places, lived frugally. When they needed a new outbuilding or corral they went to the mountains and cut the trees or poles needed to build it. They relied on their ingenuity and hard work to provide for their families.

If barns and outbuildings were not on good foundations, the men could haul manure and bank it around the bottom logs to make them snug for the winter. Although some builders used clay daubing, a good many relied on cowpies as a natural caulk. It was a ready-made plaster that could be utilized almost every morning after turning the milk cows out of the barn for the day. The pungent substance worked fine until summer came when it would dry and fall from the cracks. With a constant supply from the cows within the barn, the families could easily redaub buildings with manure whenever the need arose.

The use of cowpies to caulk and seal the buildings wasn't restricted to barns as the homesteaders, with no real alternative, used it on their homes as well.

As the summer sun rose and fell over the Gros Ventre and Teton ranges, the work turned to harvesting hay using a contraption called a "Mormon Derrick." The men would cut the crop in the field and pitch it onto a horse-drawn wagon to be hauled to the stack. The Mormon Derrick was at the location chosen for the hay to be stored in a loose pile.

The derrick was a framework of logs with a pyramid of lighter poles about twelve feet high. A bolt held a taller log in place up through the center of the pyramid. The resulting forked device had four half-curled iron bars, called teeth, used to catch the hay and transfer it to the stack.

The Mormon Derrick method of stacking worked, but it was hard back-breaking labor and time consuming. The homesteaders eventually replaced the derrick with a beaver slide stacker that was about twelve to fifteen feet high and constructed of long poles sloping at a forty-five degree angle and about twelve feet wide. They hauled hay to the stacker and pushed it up in front of the beaver slide. Then a separate device known as a plunger and powered by a big, steady team of

Stacking hay with a beaver slide using a tractor driven by Judy Moulton rather than a team of horses to move the load to the top of the stack. (Photo Credit: Clark and Veda Moulton Collection)

horses literally pushed the hay up the beaver ramp. It tumbled over the top of the slide to land in a sweet-smelling heap that grew quickly to form a stack.

Late summertime found the men in the field harvesting plump oats. Threshing was a major job requiring the labor of many men and boys. The process started when the men cut the grain in the patches and gathered it into sheaves which they tied together with twine and left standing upright in the field. In later years a binder cut and gathered the grain stalks.

As harvest started, a team-pulled wagon moved across the land so the men could load the bundles of grain. They hauled the sheaves to the hardwood threshing machine at the May homestead. The feeder was a high platform where a man stood in the center and hand-fed or pushed the sheaves of grain into the whirling cylinder. That started the threshing action which separated the grain from the straw and chaff.

Grain shocks on land east of the Mormon Row lane. Because of the productivity of the area, considerable debate ensured over whether it should be included in Grand Teton National Monument (Photo Credit: Clark and Veda Moulton Collection)

One man fed the sheaves into the machine while two other men, or more often a couple of boys, used short pieces of fork handles with a serrated binder section riveted to the end to cut the string holding the bundles together. Although the youngsters involved in the operation had the joy of being part of the crew, the tedious action of drawing the serrated binder section across the string to cut it and loosen the stalks of grain was tiring. Their arms and shoulders ached so much at night that they had trouble sleeping.

While one crew hauled the grain to the threshing machine,

another group ran the water wagon routinely from the creek or ditch. They needed water to furnish the steam generated by the little engine that powered the processing machine. The faithful draft horses pulled the wagon to the source and then the men put a cylinder with a long wooden handle on it into the ditch. The men cranked the handle and filled the tank before returning to the boiler of the steam engine.

Fall harvest and a bumper crop. (Photo Credit: Clark Moulton Collection)

Operating that engine also required a substantial pile of wood for the engineer to feed the fire box and create the steam for the power. As they did during cattle roundups, neighbors joined together to share the threshing chores.

The combined hands made the work more efficient, but they also created an additional burden for the woman of the homestead where the activity took place. Wives had to prepare two and sometimes three big meals a day for the crew that never consisted of fewer than a dozen men and a complement of young boys.

Fortunately the women shared their duties, so the work didn't fall to one. Neighbors gathered willingly to prepare the food. The men killed chickens, which they left in big tubs for the women to pluck and prepare along with mountains of homegrown vegetables and potatoes. Each woman contributed her own loaf of bread and other specialties to the meals.

Complaints didn't spice the hard work of preparing a meal. The women knew threshing meant there would be feed for stock during the upcoming winter, and fresh, clean-smelling straw to put in bed ticks smashed hopelessly flat during the previous year.

Grovont School first convened in the living room of the Perry home, but when the church building was nearly done the school classes moved to the partly finished basement of that building. Eventually the homesteaders built a separate school for their children, but when it burned, classes returned to the church until a new structure could be raised. As was the case in most pioneer communities, the church was the site for other community affairs, including all funerals whether the deceased was Mormon or not.

Music was a large part of life. Not only did residents sing at the little church constructed midway down the row, but music was entertainment and enjoyment at dances regularly held in the church or the school house.

Grovont school children, about 1930. (Photo Credit: Harley Moulton Collection)

At Christmas and one or two other times during the year, students held plays and other fun activities at the church. Henrie May always furnished the necessary music. In later years his sons and grandsons played their various instruments at the local dances. The community dances sometimes became a little embarrassing for the LDS bishop to manage. Smoking was forbidden inside the building, but on occasion someone would challenge the rule and need to be ejected.

James and Nan Budge raised eight children at Grovont before they sold their homestead in 1941 and retired to a small parcel of land in Wilson. There Nan continued to keep a few horses and she made pets of the fish in Fish Creek that ran across a corner of their land. The trout came when Nan fed them scraps of meat or bread. The fish became quite tame and grew to be fat and large.

One day a man decided to try his hand at hooking a large

trout. He was successful, but soon found he'd caught a wildcat in the form of Aunt Nan Budge. She lit into him about fishing in her stream and threatened to call the police. The man, properly chastised, left the area and Aunt Nan's fish were not threatened again. Of course the fish weren't Nan's. They belonged to the State of Wyoming. But you know what they say about possession being nine-tenths of the law. Aunt Nan had control and she took care to keep it.

The eldest Budge child, William Allen, was born in 1897 in the Johnny Carnes cabin on Flat Creek where the family first lived upon arrival in Jackson Hole. Son Jim followed a year later, also making his appearance in the Carnes cabin. Not long after the two boys were born, their father completed a homestead cabin on Mormon Row and the family moved there at the southeast end of Blacktail Butte. Other children followed including Huldah, Marian, Archie, Edward, Mary, and Myrtle.

The Budge children first attended school in 1904 in a one-room cabin on the Warren Henry homestead near Kelly. A year later residents built the Grovont School and there all of the Budge children received part of their education. Some also attended the Kelly School.

The eldest son, who always went by his middle name of Allen, helped his father with the ranch and cattle, but during World War I he volunteered in the US Cavalry. After the war, he returned to Jackson Hole where he married Nellie Seaton on Valentines Day in 1921.

Allen and Nellie filed on a homestead along the Snake River about three miles north of Moose. There they made a home for their five children, selling the property in 1931 to the Snake River Land Company. After that time home was in Jackson. Allen Budge spent his entire life in Jackson Hole, except for his years of military service.

In 1975 the Jackson Hole *News* described his life this way:

Allen's life . . . has spanned the time from the earliest wagon tracks made on the sagebrush flats to the first tracks man made upon the moon. From the days of Indian pony trails to the days of jet contrails. When he was born the white settlers of the valley were wondering if they could stop the Indians from hunting without a license.

When he died some Jacksonites were wondering if they could stop jet planes landing at the airport. All with the good of the country in mind.

Eventually Nan and James Budge's second son Jim married Kelly School teacher Viola Bruce and after working on his parents' homestead for a couple of years, he worked at the Hatchet Ranch in Moran before getting an opportunity in 1927 to claim homestead land near Deadman's Bar north of Moose. There other Budge family members joined Jim and Viola, so the homesteading routine continued in their generation. They remained on the land until 1930 when it sold to eventually become part of Grand Teton National Park.

Like others on Mormon Row, the Andy Chambers family found the work load lightened by entertainment, which included dances or card parties. They held each gathering in someone's home and the families brought along the children and food enough to last for a day and a night if necessary.

For many years Andy Chambers devoted his winters to trapping along the Snake River north of Moose and along the foothills of the Tetons. He caught mink, coyote, muskrat, and martin, and on one occasion caught two otters, a somewhat

Three of Jackson Hole's early residents, from left, Aunt Nan Budge, Maggie McBride, and Cora Nelson Barber, daughter of Slough Grass Nelson. (Photo Credit: Teton County Historical Center)

rare animal in Snake River country. "Running the lines" was his favorite pastime.

The Chambers didn't have running water on their land until 1927, a full fifteen years after Andy obtained the homestead. That same year they grieved the deaths of Ida's family, the Kneedys, in the Kelly Flood. It was a year after Andy's death in 1945 before the family had electricity. In 1946, sons Roy and Reese rigged a windmill to generate electricity. Rural Electric Administration service wouldn't serve Mormon Row for another decade.

Visitors often approached Roy Chambers and his long-time friend Clark Moulton, who grew up across the road. The visitors liked to take pictures of the Moulton barn or the Chambers' homestead.

Clark Moulton recalled:

One day some of them asked Roy if they could take a picture of the old place. He said, "Heavens yes, take a picture. I was raised in that old thing and I don't want any more to do with it. My neighbor over here, Clark Moulton, will back me up. When we were little kids and lived in those old log houses the wind howled right through those cracks! It blew so hard that our folks would have to keep an eye out to bring us back across the room where we'd been playing!"

Often they ask, "Where's Slippery Lake?" So we'd show them how to get on up to Slide Lake. They'll say, "How long have you lived here?" We'll answer. "Quite awhile, our grandparents homesteaded. The Tetons were just little fellows when we come in. We watched 'em grow up!"

John Riniker's homestead at the northernmost location on the Row, was rocky soil with no water for irrigation. Before long he became discouraged and sold his property to Jackson banker and real estate developer Robert Miller. Then John moved to Kelly where he used his four-horse hitch in a logging operation.

John and his mail-order bride, Ethel, had one son, Freddy. Ethel was scrubbing clothes outside her modest home in Kelly on a May morning in 1927 when a neighbor rushed by to tell her the Slide Lake Dam had broken and that flood waters roared their way. Ethel grabbed Freddy and raced for higher ground. The flood destroyed everything they owned. Not long after that devastating day, John, Ethel, and Freddy moved to West Warren, Utah. They'd had enough of the harsh life in Jackson Hole.

George and Martha Riniker had a tough go on Mormon Row as well. Their homestead was a dry farm which made it difficult to raise enough hay and grain for their milk cows and horses. In 1918 banker Robert Miller encouraged them to buy a second ranch on the Gros Ventre River west of Kelly because it had water for crop irrigation.

To buy the land, however, they had to mortgage the homestead, to which they had clear title. Miller held the new mortgage. The new ranch of about two hundred acres was supposed to have water rights, but May Lovejoy's place was upstream from Rinikers'. She had all the water she needed, but they often did not have enough so they weren't able to put as much land into production as they earlier anticipated.

To compound the problem, the welcome end of World War I also meant an end to the booming wartime economy. The Rinikers had acquired a herd of cattle along with the property when they bought the Gros Ventre property. With inadequate water, they had to buy hay for the stock, paying the then astronomical fee of thirty-five dollars per ton. When beef prices dropped after the war, they couldn't sell the animals for enough to cover their expenses, much less make a profit.

George and Martha could barely pay their property taxes and make interest payments, let alone reduce the principal on their loan with Miller. During those years they were just treading water. Then on May 18, 1927, a major flood tore through their lives.

Besides losing much of their lamb crop in the Kelly Flood, their buildings were destroyed or severely damaged. The family returned to its Mormon Row ranch, took handouts from the Red Cross, and tried to start over.

Robert Miller foreclosed on the Mormon Row property and sold it to the Snake River Land Company—which would eventually turn it over to the federal government for a national monument and national park. Miller offered to trade George and Martha a ranch in South Park in exchange for the Gros Ventre ranch, which he also sold to Snake River Land Company.

With no real alternative and their dreams in ruins, they accepted the offer and in 1928 moved to the Timmin's ranch which they found was a rodent-infested, rundown wreck of a place. Although sons Gordon and Dale lived in the house, Martha refused to set foot in it. Instead the family pitched tents and George headed up Game Creek to cut logs for a new house.

Robert and Grace Miller strongly influenced Jackson's early growth. She platted the town and later served as the first woman mayor. He worked as the forest supervisor, was a bank owner and real estate developer. Their home, shown here, still stands just east of Jackson on the National Elk Refuge Road. (Photo Credit: Teton County Historical Center)

Tragedy and hard times weren't quite finished with the Rinikers. George had a new team of horses for the South Park ranch. One of the horses was a rodeo outlaw prior to being broken for ranch work. One day George took the team to the barn to change harnesses. As he stood behind the team to remove the harness, one of the harness buckles hit the rodeo horse in the flank.

The startled horse kicked back with both feet, striking George in the head, and crushing his skull. The family sought help, but the valley's only physician, Dr. C.W. Huff—whom many considered a miracle worker—was out of town. Two doctors on a hunting trip in the valley cared for George, but he died at the ranch about twenty hours after the accident.

Gordon Riniker, who was seventeen when the horse kicked his father, believed then that Dr. Huff could have saved his father, had he been in town. But from the wiser perspective of an adult, he now concedes that the injuries were too severe for anyone to save George's life.

Following that tragic accident, Martha's brother, Nate Davis, interceded on her behalf with banker Miller, convincing him to refund the Riniker money for the South Park ranch so she could move to town. With that money she purchased a lot in Jackson. Neighbors used the logs George had cut for a new home on the Timmin's place to build a house in town for Martha and her six children.

Son Gordon went to work hauling cattle for Bill Kelly, the man for whom the town is named. Gordon sent money home to the family and Martha started working in a cafe. Then, at the request of Dr. Huff, she began taking in women who had just had babies, assisting them for a few days. The work kept the family in food and clothes.

Although they lived on Mormon Row for eighteen years, neither George nor Martha were members of the LDS church. George came from a Lutheran family and Martha belonged to no church until her latter years. Her family was Mormon, and she attended the church as a young girl in Utah, but in 1977 she told her grandson Olan Riniker, she did not consider herself a member of the church.

Olan Riniker wrote:

During our 1977 interview she even confided to me that she doubted the existence of God. I was trying to elicit some response from her regarding her philosophy of life. She said she never thought much about such things. "I just live from day to day." Then I asked her about her religious views. She said she wasn't religious. Still persisting I asked, "Well, do you believe in the hereafter and that there is a

God?" "No, I can't say I do. Maybe I'm terrible, but I just don't."

Martha's daughter, Elaine joined the Mormon Church in the early 1980s and eventually convinced Martha to become a member as well. Martha died in 1985 in Jackson at age ninety-three.

Joe Pfeiffer lived a solitary life on a homestead that he never got around to finishing. When the movie *Shane* was filmed in the area, its production involved many Jackson Hole people. Pfeiffer wasn't a participant, but he sold two of his wagons to the film company for twenty-five dollars. "They seemed to like 'em . . . I couldn't use 'em anymore," he said.

Pfeiffer was a crusty-looking old man, balding on top when Grand Teton National Park was established. The image of him seated on a hand-hewed wooden work bench before a small log cabin at the foot of the Tetons is that of a hard-working man with the character lines to show his age. His cabin's exterior walls had wooden slat chinking and decorations of an assortment of wire, buckets, and tools.

It could have been Pfeiffer's cabin, or any of the other buildings on Mormon Row a homesteader's grandson envisioned when he penned a tribute to the homestead era.

Joe Pfeiffer's homestead. (Photo Credit: Candy Moulton)

I BEAR BLEAK WITNESS
(this is the cabin speaking)

I bear bleak witness to a Nation's past
My bones lie bleaching in the burning sun, I was not
    meant indefinitely to last,
But only to fill a fleeting moment, a period of time
And then be gone, to make way for habitat more fine.

Without me, the letter of the law could not have been ful-
    filled
And a nestor's dream of empire would have come to
    naught,
And vast expanses of our land would have remained
    untilled
A stark reminder of the futility of battles fought.

My needs are few, I ask for little
Save for the protection of a fence of buck and rail
The ravages of time only enhance my beauty blending me
    into the landscape beside a time dimmed trail.

A robin's nest beneath my eaves bespeaks my harmony
    with nature,
The frolicksome ground squirrels within my open doorway
Echo the laughter of children long since gone
And I am left with memories to haunt my waning years.

I am a gentle reminder of man's past
A time when he was not afraid to dare
And hoped the evidence of his works would last
To prove he had the decency to care.

My only hope is that the legions who tramp the avenues of
    time
Will pause in their heedless flight
And pay homage to the things that made life good and
    right.

—Lester May

Preserved for
America

Because civilization has moved into the choicest areas faster than they could be established as national parks, some parks must now be carved out of developed areas.
                              —National Park Service Director Arno B. Cammera, 1935

Mormon Row families were struggling to make land pro-ductive when World War I broke out in Europe. Although some of the boys answered the call of country and served, World War I didn't have a big effect on the self-sustaining community of Grovont. However, another happening first proposed during the war years changed life forever on the Row.

In 1915, Stephen Mather headed the national parks for the United States Department of the Interior. That August he and his top assistant, Horace Albright, took a tour of western mountains and national parks including Yellowstone. At Moran the two made a spur-of-the-moment decision to head down into Jackson Hole.

As they drove over the terrible roads into the hole the two were "just flabbergasted by the beauty, majesty and glory of those mountains across Jackson Lake," Jackson historian Lorraine Bonney said. Mather immediately started questioning why the Tetons weren't already in the national park system.

The summer of 1916 found Albright back at the foot of the Tetons with a small party of Washingtonians. They stayed at the hunting lodge of Ben Sheffield. After a dinner of thick T-bone steaks, the party went with Sheffield out onto Jackson Lake. The view of the Teton range astounded them.

"They were simply left gasping as they realized what they were looking at—a wild, beautiful country with nobody living there except a few ranchers and several dude ranches," Bonney said.

From that day on, Mather and Albright felt the area should be preserved as a national park. It would be thirty-five years before their dream would become a reality—years in which residents of Jackson Hole became sharply divided about the prospect of another national park in their neighborhood.

Mather and Albright first attempted to extend the boundaries of Yellowstone National Park so that it included the Teton Range. In 1918 Wyoming Congressman Frank W. Mondell introduced legislation to provide for that extension. July 8, 1918, President Woodrow Wilson issued an Executive Order withdrawing more than six hundred thousand acres of the Teton National Forest from development. The Forest Service loudly protested.

There was little other opposition, however, until 1919 when cattlemen started to voice concern about the effect on cattle range if the park was to be expanded. Idaho Senator John Nugent successfully stopped the process when he heard complaints from Idaho sheepmen who thought the new park boundary would extend to the Idaho state line. That wasn't the case, but Nugent's concern was enough to send the legislation down in defeat.

In July of 1919 Albright, then superintendent of Yellowstone National Park with the continued dream of extending the park boundaries, visited with Wyoming

Governor Robert D. Carey, hitting upon a plan to improve roads into the Jackson Hole area that would help boost tourism and provide better service for valley residents.

What Albright failed to realize, however, was that Jackson Hole had an influential resident in the form of two-hundred-pound Robert Miller. In 1882 Miller had first ventured into Jackson Hole as a nineteen-year-old. Three years later he returned with his family to settle permanently. By 1919 he was a leading cattleman, owner of the Jackson State Bank, a real estate developer, and Forest Service supervisor.

When Albright and Governor Carey visited Jackson to promote their plans for improved roads, they met a crowd of people who were used to and relished their isolation. As Albright explained how the park service would improve roads and build bridges, residents became hostile. The dude ranchers, led by Struthers Burt, vociferously opposed the plan, the cattlemen strongly attacked it in fear of how it would effect their grazing rights, the Forest Service expressed outrage that it would lose control, and to top it all off the governor changed his position on progress and development. Albright found himself in a stew that was just starting to bubble.

Struthers Burt told Albright, "We just don't want the public and the park in here."

After the smoke cleared, Albright had learned something from the residents of Jackson Hole. Bonney said:

> They wanted to preserve their country intact. He did too. They wanted no new roads. Neither did he. They wanted no further invasion of commercialism. He agreed. It was a new thing for Albright to find a whole community against the march of progress.

Over the next four years a flurry of activity related to development of water for irrigation projects in Jackson Hole and Idaho undertaken by ranchers and the US Bureau of Reclamation made it clear that the area at the base of the Tetons could be widely developed before long. Concern over Idaho efforts to get control of Jackson Hole water caused some to change their stand on park expansion. They also had worries about development that was cropping up along the valley of the Snake River.

By 1923, some of the opposition to park expansion had changed. Struthers Burt, who strongly opposed it earlier, now said a national recreation area might be just the thing to protect the land and keep it pristine. A year later the possibility of restricting development in the area took a leap forward when Albright learned that John D. Rockefeller would visit the Yellowstone area.

With his teenage sons John, Nelson, and Laurance, Rockefeller arrived by railroad pullman in Gardiner, Montana, where he met Albright. The park man was under strict orders from his Washington superiors not to present park problems or proposals to Rockefeller. He could, however, let the family catch a glimpse of the Teton range.

After Rockefeller returned to New York he wrote Albright and questioned him about the unsightly roadsides he had seen in Yellowstone. The park official said workers left the debris along the roads during construction and that Congress hadn't appropriated adequate funds to clean the mess. Rockefeller said he would provide the money. Over the next four years he anonymously funded the roadside cleanup.

That was the beginning of a relationship that would culminate in realization of Mather and Albright's dream of 1915 to preserve the Tetons for America.

Rockefeller became interested in the area and in 1927 the Jackson Hole purchasing plan got underway. During the next dozen years the Snake River Land Company—ironically headed by Jackson banker Robert Miller who earlier opposed park expansion—bought land along the base of the Tetons. Rockefeller provided the money for the land, but most people didn't know that until years later.

One park historian wrote:

Mr. Rockefeller's sole purpose was to insure the preservation for future public enjoyment of the Jackson Hole region, with its unsurpassed views of the Grand Teton Mountains and its unusual opportunities for the conservation and study of game.

Grand Teton National Park was established in 1929. It encompassed the mountain range, but did not extend to the broad valley east of the Snake River. Then efforts shifted to development of the Jackson Hole National Monument that would include that ground considered essential to wildlife. The proposed monument ground would include land homesteaded by John Carnes, John Holland, Jim and Nan Budge, and the many families living on Mormon Row.

The people of Jackson Hole became bitterly divided about the development of a Grand Teton National Monument. Even so the *Jackson's Hole Courier*, which supported development of the park, was prophetic in its prediction of August 21, 1930:

> From our experience have [come] the firm belief that this region will find its highest use as a playground, and in this way will eventually become the greatest wealth-producing region of the state.

The Snake River Land Company under the wheeling, dealing leadership of Miller, started its land purchases and intended to approach the homesteaders around Grovont along Mormon Row. However in November of 1929, Wyoming Governor Frank C. Emerson appealed to the company not to buy that land saying it was for the most part good soil, and well adapted to profitable farming.

A primary concern throughout the controversy that surrounded the establishment of the Jackson Hole National Monument and eventually an expanded Grand Teton National Park, was the effect on local tax revenues if so much of the property in Teton County fell under federal control. The local residents also vociferously opposed the plans because they felt like outsiders were stepping in. They feared a loss of control on their property and changes in their lifestyle.

The company responded favorably to the governor:

> We have given considerable thought to your recommendation that we eliminate from the purchasing program of the Snake River Land Company the land around Mormon Row and extending eastward to the Gros Ventre River. . . . We are willing to defer to your wishes in the matter, to leave

this property out of our purchasing program at your request, and to make no further purchases in this area at the present time, other than the few parcels we have already acquired and one or two additional parcels which we are under obligation to purchase from the present owners.

The following spring Mormon Row residents raised questions about the elimination of their lands from the purchasing plan. They appealed to Governor Emerson who met with them on the Row and who agreed to withdraw his opposition to sale of that acreage.

Although the governor personally opposed sale of the valuable agricultural land, he deferred to the wishes of the owners. Harold Fabian, vice president of the Snake River Land Company, met with Mormon Row residents at the church meeting house on the lane. Fabian reported:

I further told them that we would not again undertake the piecemeal purchase of their property and that if they desired to have their lands reincluded it would be necessary for them to agree among themselves on a lump sum price to be paid for the entire Mormon Row section.

By the spring of 1931, the company planned to request additional funding from Rockefeller for the purchase of the Mormon Row land when former governor and then-Senator Carey raised complaints of the continued activities of the company. The deal fell through.

Some Mormon Row parcels that had earlier been contracted were obtained and the Snake River Land Company purchased other places in Jackson Hole, often for the price of back taxes. After the 1927 Kelly Flood deposited boulders on fields and washed away topsoil, many ranchers were only too glad to get any offer for their land. By 1933 the Snake River Land Company had control of more than thirty-three thousand acres on both sides of the Snake River bought for an average price of thirty-nine dollars per acre.

During congressional debate over establishment of the Jackson Hole Monument, Jackson Hole's history became paramount. As Newton B. Drury, director of the National Park Service said:

> The Jackson Hole was favored by the early trappers because of its wealth of wilderness resources. . . . Jackson Hole has an important relation to the early history of this country. It is recognized by historians as one of the important scenes of two significant movements—the fur trade era and the era of frontier settlement. It remains, relatively unchanged, largely as it was when those important historic events took place.

In July of 1938, Governor Lester C. Hunt wrote the president protesting the creation of the Jackson Hole National Monument. Many other local and state organizations were on record in opposition as well. That strong resistance effectively stopped efforts to turn the area over to federal control. But Rockefeller wasn't done. He controlled thirty-three thousand acres of prime land and—supported by officials in the Park Service and Department of the Interior—was determined it should be in federal ownership.

The wrangling over expansion of the federal land control in Jackson Hole continued until March 15, 1943, when President Franklin D. Roosevelt—under pressure from Interior Department Secretary Ickes and using the obscure Antiquities Act of January 8, 1906—signed an Executive Order establishing the Jackson Hole National Monument. Located between Yellowstone National Park and the town of Jackson, and adjoining Grand Teton National Park on the east, the monument was necessary, the president said, to preserve "historic sites and features of great scientific interest."

Roosevelt's action came without the knowledge of Wyoming's governor, senators, congressmen or anyone else in the hierarchy of the state. Jackson Hole residents were furious that their democratic freedoms were so easily shunted aside. It appeared to them that the President took his action so Rockefeller could donate to the federal government the many acres of land he had acquired through the Snake River Land Company dealings.

The people of Jackson Hole said:

A history of the Park extension movement is a surprising picture of the will of a Federal Bureau and a relatively few private individuals, some of whom stand to gain personal advantages, to harass and coerce the residents of a progressive community to an extent which has seriously retarded normal development of the potentially rich resources of this region over a period of forty years.

The monument included 99,354 acres of national forest lands, 39,640 acres of land already withdrawn from the public domain, 33,795 acres of land owned by Rockefeller, 31,640 acres comprised of lakes, 1,406 acres of state school land and 16,101 acres of private land. The total size was 221,610 acres.

Many settlers fought government and Rockefeller plans for a monument. Cattlemen particularly made the headlines when they refused to abide by Jackson Hole National Monument decree that they not graze their cattle in the area.

The *Jackson's Hole Courier* reported in 1943:

In their unanimous decision to graze their stock despite any letters from the Park Service to the contrary, the Jackson Hole cattlemen threw down the gauntlet with a clang that will be heard from coast to coast.

Five thousand head of cattle are now on the monument and the Park Service be damned!

The charge was led by, among others, Clifford Hansen, whose family had long ranched in Jackson Hole and who would eventually be both Wyoming's governor and senator.

On May 13, 1943, the State of Wyoming, furious over the president's executive order and concerned about "States' Rights" filed suit challenging the validity of the Jackson Hole National Monument. Nearly two years later, on February 10, 1945, US District Judge T. Blake Kennedy called for dismissal of the suit. He wrote, "This seems to be a controversy between the legislative and executive branches of government in which the court cannot interfere."

Congress moved to rescind the president's order and the squabble continued through the decade. However, by December of 1949, Rockefeller had donated to the government his huge chunk of land in Jackson Hole and the way cleared for settlement of the controversy. Finally in September of 1950, Public Law 787 created the expanded Grand Teton National Park.

The broad valley was finally and truly preserved for America, but the cost was bitter division among Jackson Hole residents and loss of autonomy for those whose homesteads now lay within the federal confines.

Antelope Flats once again became a place for the buffalo to range free when the land became preserved for America as Grand Teton National Park in 1943. (Photo Credit: Candy Moulton)

In order for the nation to enjoy the land, the families who had turned it from sagebrush and native grasses into productive ranches, had to sell. Their lifestyle change was necessary, according to National Park Service Director Arno B. Cammera in a 1935 letter.

"Because civilization has moved into the choicest areas faster than they could be established as national parks, some parks must now be carved out of developed areas," Cammera wrote.

For many, little feeling accompanied the sale of the land. It was a period of depression in America and the offer of cash for land was too good to refuse. Heads of the families were men who had worked for decades and now were ready to take life a little easier. Their children had already left Jackson Hole, or worked at other jobs. There was little sense in hanging on to land that was going to be in a national monument or a national park.

Most took the money offered for their property with grateful, work-roughened hands. Now, they thought, they could have an easier life. One by one the Mormon Row settlers sold to the Jackson Hole Preserve or the National Park Service.

In many cases the land was sold, but leased back by the seller. Young men like Lester May, who ranched on acres that his father Henrie homesteaded, got short-term leases. Others received a life-time contract so they could remain on the land as long as they or their spouse lived.

Andy Chambers sold his land and then leased it back from the government. His property remained in the family until the early 1980s. Andy also leased property originally owned by other Mormon Row homesteaders after it became part of the park holdings.

Not all families sold quickly. The Moultons clung to the earth with all the tenacity they had shown when they first built their homestead cabins. They recalled the years and years of toil and struggle to make a better life as they hauled water from the Gros Ventre for their domestic use, for their livestock, and to nourish their gardens. They recalled the long, bitterly cold winters spent fighting to feed cattle and horses and to keep elk out of the haystacks. They remembered the wonderful times on the Row: picnics, dances, fishing, and worship in the tiny church down the lane. They recalled borrowing money during World War II to buy war bonds to support America, the country that had given them such opportunity.

Life on Mormon Row was more than a place to live. It was

The final oat threshing on Mormon Row took place September 11, 1979. (Photo Credit: Olie Riniker)

a spiritual communing with nature and a monument to hard work and dedication.

So the Moultons hung on. Wallace sold first. He'd been the brother more inclined to visit with a friend or his school-teacher wife, Katy, in the house, than to be out early in the morning taking care of his business. Wallace had intended to become a forest ranger, but the lure of free land was too strong so he became a homesteader instead.

While the other ranchers on the lane often had a kind of contest to see who could complete chores earliest, Wallace took his time. He got the work done, the cattle fed and cared for, but in his own good time. It is not surprising he was the first of the three Moulton brothers to sell to the park service.

Brother John sold his land in 1953, but he retained a life-time lease that allowed him to live on the land until his final years. After John's retirement his son Reed and grandson Bob operated the ranch. During the latter years of John's life, after Reed's death and Bob's decision to leave the area, distant cousins, Merrill and Gladys Moulton, cared for the ranch.

John eventually retired in Jackson where he died at age 103 in 1990. During August of 1991, the family members made the final trek from Mormon Row before the National Park Service took over. They carried with them family heirlooms and memorabilia collected during eighty-three years of homesteading at the foot of the Tetons.

Thomas Alma Moulton, knew better than anyone how to build a barn to withstand massive amounts of snow that fall in Jackson Hole. (Photo Credit: Harley Moulton Collection)

Alma Moulton wanted to sell in the early 1950s, but his sons, Clark and Harley, convinced him to hold on to the land for another decade, and the start of another generation.

Clark and Veda had their own Mormon Row property where they raised three children, Clark Jr., Betty, and Judy.

Work continued in all seasons with winter duties to include cutting firewood, done here by Clark Moulton and son Clark Jr., in 1943, the year Grand Teton National Park got Congressional approval. (Photo Credit: Clark and Veda Moulton Collection)

In 1936 when Clark and Veda married, the Snake River Land Company already owned most of the marginal agricultural land around Mormon Row and was beginning to purchase homesteads on the Row. Unlike many young men who grew up on Mormon Row and whose main desire was to leave the area, Clark wanted to stay there and engage in ranching with his father. Alma gave the young couple an acre of ground south of his house and barns. Clark fenced the land and went to the county attorney to get the title straight.

For the next fifty years Clark and Veda lived in the house they built on their acre of ground and made a living from operating other Mormon Row properties. They watched as their friends and neighbors and school chums sold their land and moved away. They retired in 1987, but they didn't sell their acre.

In 1994 they were the only residents of Mormon Row, their acre the only privately-owned land on the Row settled first by Veda's great grandfather, James I. May. They said they will never sell. They want the heritage of the homesteader on Mormon Row to be kept alive. The land eventually will pass to their children, the fourth generation to own property on Mormon Row.

Harley and his wife Flossie settled on Alma's homestead where the first four of their five children—Dan, Ila, Steve, and Jerry, spent part of their childhood. The three eldest attended the Grovont school where their father learned to read, write, and do arithmetic. They worshiped in the same church as their grandparents.

Harley Moulton ready to feed a load of hay with a help from the third generation on Mormon Row, his children, Danny, Ila and Steve and niece Judy Moulton. (Photo Credit: Clark and Harley Moulton)

Clark and Harley improved the ranch. They wanted their children to know the joys of living and growing up in a small, tightly-woven, caring community.

But it was not to be. In 1960 Alma sold the homestead to the National Park Service. With it went the house where Harley and Flossie were rearing their children. They packed their belongings and headed over the mountains to the south fork of the Shoshone River near Cody, Wyoming, where they bought another ranch. The sale of the Moulton homestead, like the James I. May homestead before it, marked a direct passage of land to only one owner.

Melba Moulton May recalled land transactions on Mormon Row this way:

Well, it was interesting when we [she and Lester May] bought the Budge place. The abstract was directly to the Budges from [President] Teddy Roosevelt and then to us from the Budges and then back to the Government. But my Dad's abstract was directly from the Government to him and back to the Government, there was no one in between.

Harley Moulton's four children didn't forget the early days on Mormon Row. They instilled in youngest brother, David, born after the family moved to Cody, an appreciation for the hard work and dedication and perseverance of their grandparents. All five of them took their spouses to Mormon Row soon after their marriages. It was more than a ramshackle house and a barn. The site was inspiration. It was their heritage. The legacy of their grandfather. It was a poor man's dream.

PART IV

Rough Times

An Outlaw
Here and
There

Isolated by mountain passes and a short summer season, Jackson Hole saw little use after the decline of the fur trade in the 1840s. For nearly thirty years, few men ranged into the region. There were some who refused to quit trapping, but it wasn't until the late 1870s that Jackson Hole had much use. Then a loosely-knit gang of horse thieves moved in.

The leader likely was Harvey Gleason who answered to William C. "Teton" Jackson, a name taken from the country. Gleason spent his early life in the east. He was born in Rhode Island in 1855 and had a scrape with the law in Joplin, Missouri. He may have run pack trains and scouted with

General George Crook in the 1876 campaign against Sioux
Indians in the Powder River Basin of Wyoming. He likely killed
two soldiers and escaped to Jackson Hole.

Jackson quickly gained a reputation as an outlaw. Wyoming
Sheriff Frank Canton said Jackson killed numerous deputy US
Marshals from Utah and Idaho who trailed him to Wyoming.

The Chicago *Herald* called Jackson "the premier horse-thief
of the mountains." Known for his fiery red hair, Jackson had a
stubby beard and "eyes as black as a snake," according to
Canton. Jackson and his "gang" stole horses in Nevada, Utah,
Montana, and Idaho, then took them to Jackson Hole or Teton
Basin for rebranding. When the fresh brands healed, the men
drove the horses east on into other parts of Wyoming or South
Dakota to sell them. Once there the gang reversed its operation, stealing horses, trailing them to Jackson Hole for the

President Chester Arthur visited Yellowstone National Park in 1883.
Shown here with members of his party, Arthur is seated in the center.
During his visit security was high, perhaps because of the rumor a
group of cowboy horse thieves headquartered in Jackson Hole might
kidnap the president. (Photo Credit: Teton County Historical Center)

rebranding operation, and then taking them to Idaho and points west for resale. It was a slick operation that involved many outlaws. Some reports say as many as three hundred men took part in the business, although that may be an exaggeration.

In 1884 Jackson and Harry Thompson were indicted for murder after they crossed snow-covered Teton Pass in February 1884 to report the death of Robert Cooper to authorities in Eagle Rock, Idaho. Jackson and Thompson said they quarreled with Cooper, whom they killed in self-defense. A lack of evidence led to their acquittal.

A year later the *Idaho Register* in Eagle Rock [now Idaho Falls] said they stole forty head of horses from the High and Stout Ranch of Blackfoot, Idaho. A posse lit out after the outlaws only to return empty-handed three weeks later. Later that year Jackson was in jail for the horse theft, finally nabbed by Johnson County Sheriff Canton of Buffalo.

Teton Jackson remained in Buffalo's jail until October 24, when Idaho authorities arrived to take him to Bingham County for a trial. His trial soon took place and in early November 1885, Jackson found himself a prisoner at the United States Penitentiary in Boise City. Less than a year later, Jackson escaped his prison cell. He dodged the law for a couple of years before Montana authorities collared him near Billings in April 1888 with a herd of fifty-eight horses bearing thirteen different brands from Nevada ranches.

After four years in prison, Jackson received a pardon and he returned to Jackson Hole. Not long after his April 6, 1892, return to freedom a Casper reporter wrote an article based on an interview with a "hard-looking citizen" camped at Fort Caspar. The old man said:

> I am the fellow they call Teton Jackson, and as I was down this way, and one of my gang wants to let people know where he is, I sent for you.
>
> I make my home up south of the Park, near what is known as Jackson's Hole. . . . We are looked upon as horse thieves, and every horse that is stolen in the west is laid on me or my gang. . . . If we stole all the [horses] that they say we do we would be shipping two carloads a day.

All I ever do is act as a go-between. That is, I run the horses out of one locality and exchange them, and take back others, and I get half what the horses bring when they are sold.

In part because of Teton Jackson's activities, Jackson Hole became known as a hideout for outlaws and horse thieves. Of course for the operation to be a success it took feed, likely provided by some of the bachelors living in Jackson Hole. As Joe Pfeiffer put it, nobody could survive the harsh winters with livestock unless they had hay. Teton Jackson wasn't the only one who grabbed headlines with his horse stealing activities.

The Cunningham Ranch

J. Pierce Cunningham and his wife Margaret established a homestead at the north end of Jackson Hole in 1890. He built a "dog-trot" cabin, that consisted of two log boxes, joined and covered with a single gable roof. It formed a two-room log cabin with a roofed veranda in the middle. Sod covered the roof of poles and boards. The building logs went together in classic "saddle-V" notches that needed no nails or pegs to hold them into place.

In the fall of 1892, cowboys George Spencer and Mike Burnett brought a fine herd of horses to winter in the north end of the valley. They bought hay from Pierce Cunningham

Snow lays heavily upon the J. Pierce Cunningham cabin, where cowboys Spencer and Burnett had a shootout in 1892 when they were suspected of stealing horses. (Photo Credit: Teton County Historical Center)

who let them use his cabin on Spread Creek at the north end of the valley. During the winter rumors spread that the two cowboys were horse thieves. Hy Adams said he recognized their horses' brands as those of a Big Horn Basin rancher, for whom he had previously worked. Montana ranchers, no doubt with some justification, had voiced the opinion for many years that Jackson Hole was just a hideout for horse thieves.

The wheels of justice started turning and in April four men from Montana, and one from Idaho snowshoed over Teton Pass. They purported themselves to be deputy sheriffs, but they weren't *bona fide* sheriffs in Montana or Idaho and definitely had no jurisdiction in Wyoming. Nevertheless they "deputized" a few citizens to make a posse of a dozen and headed for Spread Creek.

One of the Jackson men "deputized" was John Holland—named as a gang member in Teton Jackson's earlier horse thievery ring and one of the first permanent settlers in Jackson Hole. Some say his position in the posse was to give it the "edge of legality."

Holland later became a Justice of the Peace in Jackson Hole and Robert E. Miller—the first forest supervisor, banker and husband of the first woman mayor of Jackson—became constable. Some say Miller also helped with the horse thievery of Teton Jackson.

Regardless of their authorization, seven members of the posse were in the Cunningham barn at daylight April 15, 1892. The other five watched the house when Spencer, known by the lawmen as one of the best cowboys in the state of Montana and a dead shot, came out of the cabin wearing his six-shooter.

As he approached the stables, Spencer heard, "throw 'em up." He started shooting instead and fell to the ground riddled with bullets. Burnett came out of the cabin with a rifle and revolver. When ordered to give himself up by those hiding outside the house, he taunted the posse and was immediately shot. The posse wrapped the "rustlers" in horse blankets and buried them in a single grave on the south side of a draw southwest of the cabin. Cunningham's partner "Swede" Jackson and Ed Hunter were in the cabin with Spencer and Burnett. Although Hunter took a shot or two at the posse, he and Jackson weren't implicated in the suspected horse thievery so they went free.

What probably really happened at the Cunningham cabin is the posse suspected two cowboys of horse rustling and the cowboys—who may or may not have been guilty, but who knew the law of the range demanded horse thieves be hanged—came out gunning for freedom, only to die in the dirt.

Deadman's Bar

Men seeking quick fortune, and sometimes fame, explored Jackson Hole looking for gold or other precious minerals. Although they generally found little, they left behind evidence of their work. The Ditch Creek ditch, which provided water to Mormon Row homesteads, got its start in a placer mining operation in 1870.

The 1889 mining operation on Whetstone Creek was the largest enterprise of its type within Jackson Hole. The company developed a giant sluice box that was supposedly designed so the gold would settle in pockets in the bottom of the box, but

159

The Snake River twists and turns at the place known as Deadman's Bar, where three men lost their lives on a mining exploration trip. (Photo Credit: Candy Moulton)

the pockets filled with pebbles and the mining company went defunct.

The most well-known of the mining operations is remembered for its gruesome remains. On a spit of land in the Snake River about midway between Moose and Moran four Germans started prospecting in 1886. The men, Henry Welter, T.H. Tiggerman, John Tonnar, and August Kellenberger, came to Jackson Hole via Butte, Montana. They visited a few days with Emile Wolff, a friend of Welter's, then left to set up an operation on the Snake. A couple of months later, Tonnar showed up at Wolff's. He spent the next three weeks helping with haying chores and said the other three men had gone hunting.

Over on that strip of land on the Snake, a Southern Pacific Railway conductor found a grisly scene while hunting and fishing. There under a pile of rocks were the decomposing bodies of Tonnar's associates. When notified, authorities arrested Tonnar, charging him with the three murders. He admitted the triple slaying, claiming he had acted in self defense. Lacking witnesses, he went free—and quickly fled the country.

The incident remains a part of Jackson Hole history with the spit of land taking the name Deadman's Bar.

Indian Hunting Conflict

In most cases the Indians and the white men of Jackson Hole's early development co-existed without much problem, but in 1895 conflict arose. The Wyoming Game Department established rules allowing hunting only part of the year, but the Bannock Indians cited 1868 treaty provisions as proof they could hunt whenever and wherever they wanted.

Chief Race Horse—whose Bannock name was Po-ha-ve— came to Wyoming where he killed seven elk. Officials arrested the chief and the case went to the judge who released Race Horse saying Wyoming laws were invalid against the treaty rights of the Indians. But the good news was short-lived. The

Wyoming attorney general appealed the case to the US Supreme Court, which reversed the lower court ruling and found that Race Horse and his Bannock relatives had to abide by the laws of the state.

Both Shoshone and Bannock Indians protested the decision and continued hunting. The settlers in Jackson Hole, who were coming to rely on guiding wealthy hunters in their valley, felt threatened by the Indians' refusal to stop hunting and obey the Wyoming laws. A posse from Jackson formed and headed for the Hoback and the Indian camp. The Shoshonis separated themselves from the Bannocks and headed toward Fort Washakie. As usual they opted for a peaceful resolution to a perceived crisis. Even so, the posse arrested the Shoshonis and took them to Jackson for a trial, which never took place because they told authorities where to find the Bannock camp.

A different posse then headed back up the Hoback Canyon where the Bannock arrests took place without incident, although Battle Mountain got its name in the process. As the combined posse and Indian party made its way back to Jackson, a melee erupted and unfounded news reports quickly blared that the Indians had rioted and that there was a massacre. Nothing of the sort happened, though the Indians did break away from the posse. Even so tensions were high that summer. Settlers already in Jackson Hole "forted up" at several locations and incoming whites moved cautiously as they trickled over the passes to claim land.

PART V

Guides and Dudes

Leigh and Jenny Lakes

Two of the lovely mountain lakes that attract visitors in Grand Teton National Park get their names from a mountain man and his Shoshone wife. Theirs is a tragic story.

Richard Leigh spent his childhood in England, but came to America as a boy. He eventually landed in Idaho where he started trapping. His entrance into the mountain man game in the late 1840s came as the fur era climaxed in the West. But his two abnormally large front teeth, combined with his ability as a trapper, gave Leigh the mountain name "Beaver Dick." Indians called him "The Beaver."

Leigh had a beautiful flowing script and kept a journal

167

most of his years in the Rocky Mountains and Jackson Hole. In one he wrote:

> i am the son of Richard Leigh formerly of the Britesh navey and grand son of James Leigh formly of the 16 lancers england. i was borne on Jenury 9th in 1831 in the city of Manchaster England. come with my sister to philadelphia u s a when i was 7 years old. went for the Mexcin war at close of 48 atched to E coy [company] 1st infentry 10 months when come to rocky mountons and here i die.

Beaver Dick married a Shoshone Indian woman, Jenny, with whom he had five children. He often guided prominent and well-to-do sportsmen from the East on hunts in Jackson Hole. Those men remained his friends, encouraged him in his journal-keeping, and sent magazines and pictures for him and Jenny to enjoy.

Beaver Dick and Jenny Leigh with three of their children. (Photo Credit: American Heritage Center/UW)

In 1872 when the Hayden Survey pushed into northwestern Wyoming, Beaver Dick acted as guide. That party named the mountains, and gave immortality to Beaver Dick and Jenny when they named the lakes. William Henry Jackson, the first great photographer of the West, took the only known photographs of Beaver Dick, Jenny, and their children. Jackson spent one day, as he put it, "photographing Dick's Indians." It wasn't long before the family picture altered.

In the fall of 1876 Beaver Dick and his family assisted an

Indian woman and her child. Some members of the woman's family had died and others had little lumps on their face, Leigh wrote in a letter to a friend. The woman told Leigh she was pregnant, so he "told my wife to give hur our lodge and some provishons and let her camp in the bushis [with] my Wife and children keeping away from [the woman] untill she took in labor."

Leigh, his son, Dick Junior, and a friend, Tom Lavering, went hunting and camped out one night that fall. When they returned, they found the woman had died. Later Beaver Dick wrote:

> when we got home we went and examined the womon and could see nothing suspisus about hur and come to the concluson that she had died in child bed. i asked my wife to take the little indan girle to the house and wash and clene it. she sade not to do it. somthing told hur that she wold die but at my request she took it to the house and cleaned it up. it played with my children for 4 days as lively as could be and that night it broke out all over with little red spots

Before long, Leigh's pregnant wife and children became ill. Jenny gave birth to her fifth child December 16, 1876, but the baby apparently died that day and Jenny the next. Then in rapid succession Beaver Dick lost his family to the scourge of small pox. Daughter Ann Jane, age six died December 24; William, age four died December 25; Richard Jr., age ten died December 26; and Elizabeth, age two, died December 28.

Leigh buried his family at the mouth of the Teton River. He marked each grave with a carved headboard including the name, age, and date of death. Some time later Leigh went to Fort Hall, Idaho, where he married a Bannock woman, Susan Tadpole. He built a new cabin on Leigh Creek, near the mouth of the canyon, and started another family including daughters Emma and Rose, and son William.

In 1888—having lost one family and started another—Beaver Dick guided western novelist Owen Wister through Jackson Hole and Yellowstone. Beaver Dick died March 29, 1899, at age sixty-eight.

Owen Wister,
an Early Dude

Western novelist Owen Wister, who became famous for *The Virginian*, was one "dude" in Jackson Hole prior to 1900. Many stories circulate about his writing. Old timers claim to have been the character upon which he based *The Virginian*. The book is the stuff of legends and many of Wister's scenes are in Wyoming spots like Medicine Bow, the Goose Egg Ranch near Casper, the Occidental Hotel in Buffalo, or from incidents that took place during his trips to Jackson Hole.

Wister spent a considerable amount of time in Wyoming after 1885 when his health broke down and his doctor S. Weir Mitchell, advised him to head west. Wister first visited Jackson

Hole in 1887 on a big game shooting trip. His daughter Frances Stokes wrote in a letter January 29, 1958:

> I went to Jackson Hole as a child with my parents and sister and brothers in the summers of 1911 and 1912. In 1912 we built a 2 story log cabin in the 100 acre ranch my Father bought not far from the JY [dude ranch]. . . . It was called the Owen Wister cabin and my friend told me that it was now said that Owen lived there while writing *The Virginian*. Of course none of this is true. *The Virginian* first came out in *Harper Magazine* starting as short stories in 1894 and several [chapters] came out in the [*Saturday Evening*] *Post*. It was published as a book in 1902 and my Father spent the winter 1901–1902 as the book came out in May living in Charleston, South Carolina, while he was making the short stories into the novel.

The University of Wyoming in Laramie has Owen Wister's pencil-written diaries of his time in the West and also the only two pages of pencil manuscript of *The Virginian* that exist, according to Stokes' letter.

Mitchell's son, Dr. John K. Mitchell, was a cousin and good friend of Wister. The two spent time together in Jackson Hole. Portions of a diary published in the Jackson Hole *Guide* in 1965, chronicle a trip Wister and Mitchell took in Jackson Hole.

Mitchell describes Owen Wister as D., or Dan. Wister's father wanted to name his son Daniel, but his mother preferred the name Owen. They compromised. Christened Owen, both parents called him Dan.

The more-than-a-month-long trip Wister and Mitchell took included time at Sheep Creek, known as Dick's Basin for Beaver Dick Leigh, Brooks Lake, and in Yellowstone and the Absaroka Mountain Range. Mitchell wrote:

> Monday, [August] 31st. D. and I rode to the Snake R. ferry "Jones's Ranch," to hunt up a J. P. and get a Wyo. game license for me. Across the swamp, the same troublesome swamp, we got safely enough, the trail taking the far side of the stream we had tried so often to cross, forded the

Snake, more swamp and wet willows, deep mud-holes, and presently emerged on a beautiful meadow, and struck the wagon road, down which our pack came.

We inquired for Beaver Dick [Leigh] who had left now. He was with a prospecting party of New York, and he'd be back. We cantered on, crossed Arizona Creek and all along had a most splendid view on our right of the Teton range, Mt. Moran and the 3 Tetons hanging over the head of Jackson's lake. Great fields of snow, deep sharp-cut dark valley, and bare expanse of clear gray rock alternate on their sides . . .

. . . Our route led past the ford where Robt. Roy Hamilton was drowned. His partner, Sargent, lives on the road and relates fate to all and sundry. All Jackson's Hole, a community of scalawags, renegades, discharged soldiers and, as Capt. Anderson, calls them, predestined stinkers, unite in the belief that Sargent killed H. [Hamilton]

Owen Wister frequently spent time in Jackson Hole after his first visit in the 1880s for his health. Although some like to claim that he wrote *The Virginian* while living in Jackson, his daughter said the stories for that book first appeared in magazines and he revised them and wrote the book while living in South Carolina. (Photo Credit: Teton County Historical Center)

At Jone's (sic) no Justice—but a good looking young
fellow, sturdy, blue-eyed and pleasant, of whom we purchased cornmeal; he invited us to stay and grub and the
promise of fresh meat was too attractive to be missed, so
we stayed and ate elk meat in the house of the game pro-
tector and justice of the peace two days before the season
opened.

Wister and Mitchell left a message for the justice of the
peace that they needed a hunting license and then set out looking for Beaver Dick Leigh who would show them the hunting
ground.

Mitchell resumes the tale:

In the edge of the swamp, 3 miles from our camp, Beaver
Dick and his prospecting party (2 gentlemen of about 50)
were making camp, assisted by B.D.s wife, an Indian, a
strapping girl his daughter and 2 or 3 small fry. A round
shouldered, long-bearded, big nosed old man, with a clear
light blue eye, is B.D—50 odd years in U.S., nearly 50 in
the Rockies, and drops his H's like a hansom cabby in the
Strand; has married 2 squaws, a Bannock and a Shoshone,
so has endless Indian friends and relations. . . ; very talka-
tive, like all the mountain men and old trappers; 28 years
scout, guide and interpreter for the Army, trapper, pioneer,
and real frontiersman, hating the encroachment of settle-
ments, and keeping away from them, till now he is getting
too old and has to spend his winters in a house, but pack-
ing his ponies and starting out every summer with his wife,
two girls and a boy, living 3 or 4 months in the Teton
range.

He is to come tomorrow and show us how to get
through the canyon without wings!

Sept. 3rd, Beaver Dick appeared today—on a
raw-boncd 3 year old cayuse, for which he had "traded" the
night before.

We climbed and scrambled, we dodged under
half-falled trees and circumnavigated trunks too high to
jump. . . . Half way down a big flat rock stuck out over the
creek at a sharper angle than the rest of the slope, and

round it we went very gingerly, as to slip on it would have shot one into the creek. At the bottom of the slope we crawled gingerly over a mass of tumbled granite rocks, all sharp edged as knives, and of sizes from a small house downward . . . [soon] Dick was scrambling up another steep bank, his one spur working viciously. Then we dropped into the stream, and went 40 or 50 yards in the water, crossed again, belly deep, at the foot of a beautiful rapid and struggled up another hill, I on foot, but Dick still in the saddle.

The party traveled another three hours up and down the steep canyon walls, before reaching an open valley where they set up a permanent camp. From that camp they explored the basin under Leigh's guidance. Riding to learn the country so they would know the way out by following the Conant Trail, the hunting party made it to the Absaroka Mountains east of Yellowstone to look for game. Mitchell said, "Dan had found and shot a ram, his bullet going thro' one horn; the ram bolted and would have escaped but West, who was 'round a corner' got a second shot in and killed him."

Wister often spent time in Jackson Hole. In a letter to Fritiof Fryxell November 26, 1929, he wrote:

That region is the country I have loved best in the world. Were there any part of my life I would live again, it would be the time spent there.

In 1888, from camp between String and Jenny Lake, at the edge of the pines where the creek enters them for its final descent into Jenny Lake, I climbed to that rocky scoop where the real steepness of the Grand Teton begins—and came down again ingloriously.

Like others who enjoyed the natural beauty of Jackson Hole, Wister supported development of Grand Teton National Park. To Fryxell he said:

Many a time I told Roosevelt that whole place should be a Park, and he quite agreed.

Signal
Mountain

Signal Mountain, at the southeast edge of Jackson Lake, got its name in 1891 after residents searched for Robert Hamilton, who is said to have lost his way while stalking game. Rescuers agreed to light a signal fire on the summit of the mountain when they found Hamilton. Nine days passed before the fire burned.

Searchers found Hamilton's body in the Snake River, two miles downriver from the Jackson Lake outlet. Jackson Hole residents always debated the cause of his death. Though some said he died accidentally, speculation that his business partner killed him filtered across the valley and the years.

Hamilton, a great-grandson of Alexander Hamilton, reportedly moved to Jackson Hole to flee a New York actress's breach of promise suit. He joined forces with John Sargent, the black sheep of a wealthy Maine ship-building family, who supposedly was a remittance man paid to stay in the West. The two men wanted to start a lodge and they called their ranch Merry Mere.

Tie-hacks from Ashton, Idaho, whipsawed the logs and pegged the corners together for a ten-room log building on Jackson Lake. The Merry Mere operation, which likely was the first dude ranch in Jackson Hole, had a short existence, in part because of Hamilton's death. Although the official story is that Hamilton drowned accidentally while hunting, some claim Sargent murdered him by sending him into a dangerous ford in the Snake River.

Besides the speculation of violence between Hamilton and Sargent, other stories circulated. In 1890 Sargent left Jackson to get his wife, Adelaide, and their children, bringing them to the valley over the Conant Trail, which crosses the Tetons about six miles north of Jackson Lake. Sargent built a store near his cabin, but he seldom stuck around to tend to business, often leaving a note instructing people to pay for anything under a dollar and to charge more expensive items.

In the fall of 1892 Sargent wrote of taking his family out of Jackson Hole, over Conant Pass to Idaho and eventually to Utah to spend the winter. He chronicled a three-day trip through a winter blizzard with his youngest daughter, Martha, then age four, and of how he cared for her as they crossed the snowy pass.

In 1897 violence again seeped into stories about Sargent. That May a party of soldiers on skis enroute from Yellowstone heard a woman's screams as they passed the Sargent place. They knocked on the window, but no one appeared, so they reported what they'd heard to authorities in Jackson. Constable Bill Manning, D.C. Nowlin, and Mrs. Sam Osborne went to the Sargent place where they found Mrs. Sargent badly beaten. They loaded her onto a sled and took her to Jackson where she died on her birthday, May 15, 1897.

Irate citizens threatened to lynch Sargent, but he disappeared and didn't return to Jackson Hole until two years later. Then he was tried and acquitted on murder charges.

In 1906 Sargent married Edith Drake, whom he met in New York. Rumor and speculation about Edith's mental state resounded through the valley with stories that she'd wander naked through the forest with only a pair of mittens on her feet. Some claimed Sargent took her clothes and she had no alternative to nudity. Others said Sargent got payments to take care of her. Sargent himself said her life "has been as full of sorrow and wrongs as my own."

Edith eventually returned to live in a New York mental institution. In the spring of 1913, Sargent put the record "God and Now We Die" on his victrola, sat before his fireplace, and shot himself with his Sharps rifle, ending the pattern of violence at Merry Mere.

Edith Sargent may have found solace in her music at Merry Mere, the isolated Jackson home she shared with husband John. Their lives were steeped in violence and tragedy. (Photo Credit: Teton County Historical Center)

Bring on the
Dudes

As early as 1890, John Sargent and Robert Hamilton envisioned a deluxe dude ranch on the shores of Jackson Lake at the north end of Jackson Hole. They built a ten-room log house and called it Merry Mere, but of course fate stepped in with the death of Hamilton and the business didn't thrive. In about 1900 Herb Whiteman and his partner built a cabin north of Jackson Lake with a similar purpose in mind, but they found the transportation of supplies both difficult and prohibitive and were forced to abandon their plans.

Before 1910, however, Ben Sheffield ran a camp for hunters and fishermen near Moran. Many working on the Jackson Lake

Dudes will do
almost anything as
this picture shows.
It is often called
the "original
mixed drink."
(Photo Credit:
Teton County
Historical Center)

Dam stayed with Sheffield and his lodge later played a role in
the creation of Grand Teton National Park when John
Rockefeller stayed there on his first trip to the region. The JY
Ranch, opened in 1908 by Henry Steward, and the Bar BC,
started by Struthers Burt and Dr. Horace Carncross in 1910,
began the real dude operations in Jackson Hole.

Early visitors to Jackson found a different style community
than those of the 1990s. Jackson historian Elizabeth Hayden
said the dudes who came to Jackson in 1910 found the town
square boxed in by log and false-front stores and a few
stretches of board walk. Hayden wrote:

> They bought their necessities at the mercantile store of Roy
> and Frank Van Vleck or at "Pap" Deloney's general mer-
> chandise, their drugs at "Doc" Steele's, ate their lunch at
> "Ma" Reed's hotel, and stopped for a quick one at Rube
> Tuttle's saloon.

Currently, trendy shops, art galleries, and specialty restaurants mix with the old-west style atmosphere of board sidewalks and cowboy bars complete with a neon bucking bronc on the roof and saddle seats at the bar.

Dude ranching started early in Jackson Hole and continues in the 1990s. Here a group of dudes "top rail" at the Triangle X Ranch as cowboys push a group of cattle out of the corral. (Photo Credit: Teton County Historical Center)

A pause at the top of the hill before descending into Jackson Hole after a cattle roundup. (Photo Credit: Teton County Historical Center)

PART VI

Looking Forward

Let the
Women Rule

Local residents believe Jackson is the first town in the nation to have a woman mayor and an all-woman council when five women took charge in 1920. Grace Miller was a two-to-one winner over Fred Lovejoy for the mayoral seat. Others elected were Rose Crabtree and Mae Deloney, two-year councilwomen, and Genevieve Van Vleck and Faustina Haight, one-year councilwomen.

For Mrs. Crabtree the victory was close to home since she defeated her husband, Henry. He didn't begrudge her the job and told reporters she had done a good job in running the

Jackson claims to be the first town in the United States to have an all-woman town council. The women were elected May 11, 1920 and served from June 1920 until June 1923. The council included, from left, Mae Deloney, Rose Crabtree, Mayor Grace Miller, Faustina Haight and Genevieve VanVleck. (Photo Credit: Teton County Historical Center)

Crabtree Hotel as his wife, so he felt she was competent to run the town.

Newspapers across the nation remarked on the election. The New York *Sun* said the "sole issue was that of sex and the two gun man didn't stand a chance with his wife and her rolling pins." A Boston paper reported, "Governor Calvin Coolidge in an address yesterday referred to the action of the citizens of Jackson, Wyo., in electing women to all town offices and paid a high tribute to the good sense of the people of the town."

Of her election, Mayor Miller told reporters:

We were not campaigning for the office because we felt the need of pressing reforms. The voters of Jackson believe that women are not only entitled to equal suffrage, but they are also entitled to equality in the management of government affairs.

Not only were Jackson's elected officials women, but the town's appointed positions also went to females. Pearl Williams Hupp took over as marshal, Marta Winger became town clerk, and the town's health officer was Edna C. Huff, the wife of Dr. Charles Huff. In the town minutes she is referred to as "Mrs. Dr. Huff."

The women didn't let any time slip by. They met to discuss plans for their administration as soon as they officially took office. They focused first on city finances. When they took office the town had about $200, but within two weeks there was about $2,000 in the treasury because they collected unpaid debts.

With finances in hand, the women then set to work on other concerns: stagnant water, no garbage disposal system, narrow culverts across the various ditches in town, and an unsightly cemetery. The women started to spend the $2,000 they had collected as new culverts went in the ditches. They passed health laws making it a misdemeanor to put garbage in the streets or on vacant lots.

The town leaders organized a clean-up week, and then gathered up the refuse and hauled it out of town where they established a permanent dumping spot. They had the streets graded, and built board sidewalks to replace pioneer trails. Finally, attention went to the cemetery. The old site got a face lift with a new fence, stones to mark the graves, and a road up the steep hillside.

National
Elk Refuge

Just outside Jackson's north boundary is the National Elk Refuge—home to the world's largest free-ranging elk herd. It is on land originally claimed by Johnny Carnes and John Holland (called Government Ranch by old timers in Jackson Hole).

Stephen Leek was a bachelor living in Jackson Hole in 1889 when the Wilson families arrived. Leek eventually married Nick Wilson's daughter and made his mark on Jackson Hole through his interest in the scenery and game of the area. He took photographs and went on the lecture circuit to describe the plight of the wild animals when they began starving to death due to lack of natural feed.

S.N. Leek, often called Jackson Hole's "Winter King" feeds elk near Jackson. His photographs and other efforts helped with the development of a regular elk feeding program. (Photo Credit: Wyoming State Museum)

It was through Leek's efforts that the elk became permanently protected. Elk feeding along Flat Creek started during the severe winter of 1908–1909, when about twenty thousand elk in Jackson Hole were starving. Valley residents raised a thousand dollars to buy hay and the Wyoming State Legislature appropriated $5,000 to purchase additional feed.

In answer to an appeal from the Wyoming State Game Warden, the US Bureau of Biological Survey helped feed the big herds through the next year and in 1912 Congress set aside a thousand acres as a winter refuge. With increased governmental appropriations and donations from national sportsmen's organizations, the refuge expanded to its present acreage. The twenty-four thousand acre tract of meadow and

Elk ate the hay they could reach in ranchers' haystacks, but it wasn't enough to save them. Photos like this one by Stephen Leek helped draw attention to the plight of the animals and ultimately led to establishment of the National Elk Refuge in 1912. (Photo Credit: Teton County Historical Center)

foothill land just north of Jackson now is winter home to between seven and twelve thousand elk that migrate annually from Yellowstone National Park, the Bridger-Teton National Forest, and Grand Teton National Park.

Initially, workers harvested hay from the meadowland in summer and fed additional concentrated foods, including cottonseed cake. By 1943 the refuge accommodated an average of ten thousand elk, but by the 1990s that figure had dropped to about eight thousand head per year. Then crews didn't harvest

Up to 8,000 head of elk winter on the National Elk Refuge just north of Jackson each winter. (Photo Credit: Steve Moulton)

the hay from the meadows, but let the grasses cure in the fall, to provide forage for the elk until actual feeding operations start, usually in January. Game personnel feed high-protein alfalfa pellets in the largest wildlife feeding program in the United States.

In 1921 the Elk Refuge also became a refuge for all species of birds. The National Elk Refuge is one of the spectacular one-of-a-kind natural tourist attractions in Jackson Hole. Horse-drawn sleighs haul visitors around and through the huge herd during the wintertime so people can observe the natural winter habits of wildlife. The area is home to more than elk since Rocky Mountain Big Horn Sheep, many species of birds, including Trumpeter Swans, and predators like coyote and fox live on the refuge as well.

In wintertime hundreds of bull elk feed along the highway north of Jackson. Most cows and calves segregate themselves in the center of the range. Some leave refuge grounds and wander into town, like a cow in the winter of 1993 that spent a few days on the porch of the Wildlife of the American West Art Museum, which then had its operations in downtown Jackson. Some tourists didn't realize the elk was alive until she shook her head or stamped a foot if they approached too closely.

Menor's Ferry

Before the Snake River had any dam across its bosom, it ran wide, fast, and turbulent through Jackson Hole. Crossing the Snake, the "accursed mad river," as the Frenchmen called it, required skill and bravado. At least that was the case before Bill Menor happened on the scene.

Tall, thin Menor spent his early life in Ohio, and came to Wyoming in 1892 squatting on the west bank of the Snake River. In 1894 he started construction of a low log house among the cottonwoods along the bank of the river, had a cow or two, some chickens, and a horse. The hard-talking Menor built a blacksmith shop, planted a garden, and plowed a field.

Bill Menor built a ferry across the Snake River and sold supplies at his store to homesteaders and tourists. (Photo Credit: Teton County Historical Center)

He eventually opened a store there on the shore of the Snake where he sold fishhooks, tin pans, groceries, and Bull Durham.

Bill Menor, being an early-day entrepreneur, built a ferry across the unreliable Snake. It was the first ferry. A second ferry later went in at Wilson. Constructed as a railed platform on pontoons, Menor's ferry moved across the river propelled by the current and guided by ropes attached to an overhead cable. On either side of the river a massive log, called a "dead-man" secured the cable. Menor's ferry was large enough to hold a four-horse team if the leaders were unhitched and held beside the wagon.

When the Snake was running bank-full and raging, Menor's ferry was the only crossing place in a forty mile stretch—practically the length of Jackson Hole. If the river was running too full, Bill wouldn't risk his ferry. Then in the early days, there was no safe crossing at all in the lower end of the Hole. People had to go to Moran where they could cross a toll bridge. Menor's ferry crossed the Snake near Moose just north of the present Grand Teton National Park Visitor's Center.

Bill knew the Snake's foibles and the power of the water. Once a huge, uprooted tree swept against the ferry with such force that the ropes broke, carrying the ferry—and Menor who was on board—downstream some distance before it grounded on a submerged sandbar. Neighbors rushed to the rescue as the ferryman cursed them and the river for his predicament.

Menor's younger brother, Holiday, also eventually settled on the banks of the Snake River in Jackson Hole. Upon his arrival in 1905, Holiday lived with Bill. Soon Holiday moved out of Bill's house to claim land on the east shore of the Snake.

During the wild berry season in late summer, Bill charged "huckleberry rates" to local people wanting to cross on his ferry. That called for fare one way to cross the Snake when the berries dripped with juice along the ridges and around the lakes under the Tetons. Holiday liked berry season, too. He canned up to sixty quarts of huckleberries every year. He used the berries—and prunes, beets, raisins, or anything else that was handy—to make a little home brew. He called it wine, but seldom gave it time to mature.

When fall turned to winter in Jackson Hole, Bill took his

Although this ferry load includes an automobile, much of the traffic using Bill Menor's ferry was wagons. The ferry was large enough to haul a wagon and four-horse hitch, as long as the lead team of horses was unhitched and held along side. (Photo Credit: Teton County Historical Center)

ferry from the river. From that time until he resumed operation in the spring, horses had to ford the river. People on foot could cross on a little platform car. They boarded and sat down, then Bill released the car. With a quick movement it ran down the slack cable to within feet of the river. The passengers then hauled themselves up the cable to the opposite bank.

Eventually Menor and his neighbors built a winter bridge across the river. Neighbors up and down the river, who might want to cross the river before the ferry was back up and running in springtime, readily gathered to put the log bridge in place in the fall. The story was different in the spring when it came time to remove the logs from the river. With the ferry back in operation and crops to plant, men who helped build the bridge in the fall couldn't find the time to remove it in the spring.

Finally one spring only one man helped Bill and Holiday Menor move the bridge. Logs too heavy for the small crew to remove got a push into the river, and that was the last season for a winter bridge.

In 1918, Bill Menor sold his ranch and his ferry to Maud Noble and Frederick Sandell. Menor said he had had enough of high water and low water, of fog, wind, rain, and snow, but he didn't seem able to drag himself from the banks of the Snake. He paced a floor no longer his, and cursed when a meal wasn't ready. Finally he packed his bags and left for California. Holiday eventually followed him there.

By 1927, a huge steel truss bridge spanned the Snake not far from the Menor houses. The ferry was beached.

Moose, which is now park headquarters, took its name from the animals who frequented the Snake River bottom land in that area. The "settlement" that had gone by the name Menor's Ferry for three decades, became Moose when the postal department required a shorter name for the post office it intended to establish there.

In 1923, an historic meeting took place in Noble's home, called the Ferry Ranch. There the first discussions took place about attracting a philanthropic group or individual to acquire privately owned lands in the valley, to preserve as a scenic, recreational, historical, and inspirational location for the people of America.

Noble and Sandell sold their property in 1929 to the Snake River Land Company, predecessor to Jackson Hole Preserve, Incorporated. Eventually it went to the National Park Service. The old cable that pulled the ferry across the river countless times, swung aimlessly across the current while the pontoon boats that supported the ferry platform lay abandoned and rotting on the river bank.

Twenty years later, in 1949, the Jackson Hole Preserve reconstructed the ferry. It relied on old photographs, the remnants of the original pontoon boats, and the memories of countless old timers to make an accurate recreation of the once-bustling ferry crossing.

The Menor homestead house is original, though restored. Initial construction took place in three phases with the west wing built in 1894, the frame central wing about a year later, and the large east wing built in 1905. The west wing served as living quarters for Menor with a bedroom and sitting room. The large central wing was the kitchen and pantry and Menor used the east portion for his store.

Menor built his cabin of locally available timber and rough-sawn boards. He whitewashed the entire building with lime he got from his brother, who mined it nearby. The reconstructed ferry and the old white-washed cabin, is a memorial to Menor.

Chapel of the Transfiguration

Just across a paved parking lot from Menor's Ferry is the log Church of the Transfiguration built in 1925. Maud Noble donated land for the chapel after she heard dudes on nearby ranches wanted to attend worship services, without the need to make the long trip into Jackson. Funding for the log church came from the various dude ranches.

The Episcopal Church owns it and named it for the Transfiguration of Christ. The grounds, set off from the surrounding flat by a buck and rail fence, are entered through a peak-roofed gate. The altar window frames the Tetons.

The Chapel of the Transfiguration served dudes in Jackson Hole.
(Photo Credit: Teton County Historical Center)

Jackson Lake Dam

The first dam on the Snake River was a log crib structure at Jackson Lake in 1906 and 1907. Its construction—at a cost of $30,203—came because of the need to store additional water for eventual use in Idaho. Engineers designed the temporary dam so it would raise the surface of the lake about ten feet, which should provide adequate irrigation water for four or five years. Between fifteen and twenty-five men helped to build that structure, which would eventually be replaced with a more permanent one.

In 1909, two engineers inspected the temporary dam and discussed plans for its replacement. On July 5, 1910, less than

Original construction of Jackson Lake Dam cost just a little more than
$30,000 as water was stored for irrigation in Idaho. When the dam was
upgraded in 1989 the price tag topped $82 million. (Photo Credit:
Teton County Historical Center)

The Jackson
Lake Dam in
1993 after an
$82 million
upgrade. (Photo
Credit: Candy
Moulton)

two weeks before irrigation deliveries would start, the log crib dam failed, releasing a flood of water that damaged bridges and one of the Snake River ferries.

An earth-filled dam was rebuilt at the site of the initial structure at a cost of $453,300. To transport materials for the dam construction, officials built a road over Squirrel Meadows, reputedly along the trail of an outlaw who took a short cut through the mountains to avoid law officers traveling the longer Marysvale road. The construction crew—some four hundred men—was twice the population of Jackson. Headquarters was at Moran, which had a hospital, four barns, an office building, and other facilities for the workers. Work on the dam continued year around. Huge fires burned in stoves to prevent the cement from freezing and a freighting crew hauled six boilers for the facility over Teton Pass through snow up to fifteen feet deep.

From 1914 to 1916, workers increased the reservoir capacity by raising the dam at its original location. The water from Jackson Lake Dam is a part of the United States Bureau of Reclamation Minidoka Project.

In 1988, the Jackson Hole *Guide* reported on a three-year project to reconstruct Jackson Lake Dam using, for the first time in the United States, new technology to increase the strength of the earthen dam's foundation. The process became necessary because of concern that the foundation could collapse during an earthquake. It didn't come cheap. The cost for the upgrade was $82 million, a far cry from the original construction tab of $30,203.

The Weathered Image

A Conclusion

May 21, 1993:

All day rain pours down in Jackson Hole. Between squalls, I slosh through mud and wet grass taking photos along Mormon Row. It is my final day on the Row this visit and I want more pictures to capture what's left of the once-thriving Grovont community.

All of the May buildings are gone, as are Rinikers, Budges, and Harthoorns. The Pfeiffer cabins and outbuildings remain, but the doors sag on broken hinges, the windows have no glass, and the roofs are falling from the weight of constant mountain snows. The Mormon church now serves as the Calico Pizza Parlor in Wilson.

At the T.A. Moulton place, only the barn remains, but it is showing definite signs of aging. The north leanto roof is falling, boards swing and sway in the wind, shingles have blown from the roof and lie as litter in the yard. John Moulton's house, barn, outbuildings, and corrals are intact, mainly because they've been abandoned only two years.

Midway down the Mormon Row lane, the Chambers buildings and Clark Moulton's one-acre holding anchor each other with the road as a dividing line. Long-since abandoned, the Chambers ranch is falling into disrepair. The loft door on the barn swings in the wind, the house is no longer liveable. The National Park Service uses the Chambers place for storage and there are piles of fence posts and equipment. Walking alone around the abandoned homestead, I try to imagine this place as a vibrant home to a large family. It's difficult and poignant. In the barn, I see the ladder up the log wall providing access to the hay loft. I consider climbing it, but reject the notion as too dangerous. These are old buildings and the boards could be rotten. It would not do to take a fall when nobody knows where I am.

Later across the road I climb into bed in one of Clark Moulton's cabins. Before I fall asleep, however, the sky lights with a jagged bolt of lightning. Several seconds later, I hear the rumbling thunder and know the flash hit miles away. With increasing rapidity, the lightning flares and the thunder rumbles, rippling and rolling through the valley of the Snake.

When it storms in the mountains, the crash and boom of thunder ricochets and cascades, bouncing from one ridge and valley to another. It is a tremendous racket.

I lie in my bed and watch lightning brighten the loft and listen to the cadence of ever increasing crashes until I can stand it no longer. I've never been able to sleep through the powerful displays of nature. High winds, blinding blizzards, jagged bolts of fire call to me. I slip down the stairs and perch on the couch looking out the picture window of this small cabin. Within seconds the heavens burst forth.

The intervals between light and sound become almost imperceptible as the night turns into an eerily lit day-time. The rapier-like streaks of fire from the sky poke and prod at the Grand Teton and its neighboring peaks.

The lightning dances through the hole and this national park once again becomes a wild wilderness. As I watch and listen, the sky flashes move toward Moran and the thunder rumbles away from my location, rather than toward it; the storm passes.

May 22, 1993:

The rutted lane is muddy. I let family members know where I will be, then I return to the Chambers homestead for one more turn around the buildings.

Like nature's display of last evening, the lure of the barn soon becomes too much for me and I climb the ladder to the hayloft. A thick layer of old dry and dusty straw and hay and the scattered bones of dead cats and calves greet me. I gaze around the loft, then gingerly inch across the floor toward the window at the north and then the door at the south. From those high vantage points, the entire Mormon Row region is visible.

I truly believe this land should remain resonant with children's laughter, women's singing, and men's whistling. Even though the Park Service owns it, the land could be in production. Ranchers could use horses for field work and keep alive the tradition of the homesteader using a beaver slide stacker and the Mormon derrick for harvesting hay.

I suspect these Chambers buildings, like others on the Row, will fall or be removed by the National Park Service.

January 6, 1994:

The power of a thunderstorm is much like the maelstrom that swept this region when the government created Grand Teton National Park. Neighbors lined up on opposite sides of the fence in that battle, which raged for nearly thirty years. Even today, conflict sometimes flares between the National Park Service and people with inholdings in the park, like the residents of Kelly who want or need to make home improvements, but who can do so only with Park Service approval.

Kelly is the only community remaining within the park, and the Park Service finds it hard to manage. As Grand Teton National Park Assistant Superintendent Melody Webb put it in December, 1993: "It's sad to see the houses go up in Kelly. It's more and more of a community, and less and less a national park." She seems to forget it was a community decades before it became a national park.

My husband's family no longer owns the Mormon Row homestead where he spent his early childhood, yet in a very real sense it is still ours.

We hate to see the deserted homesteads along the lane. At the same time, because the Park Service owns the land, now it can never become another Jackson Hole housing subdivision or condominium complex. That is important to us. This area should be forever free of further development and be a place where Americans can seek the solace of Wyoming's land. Over time, the sage will reclaim the soil, and the wide open spaces of Mormon Row and Antelope Flats will look much as they did when James I. May first rode the area in 1894.

For my children, Shawn and Erin Marie, Mormon Row is one thread in the tapestry of their life story. The legacy of their great-grandfather became the domain of a nation. Now everyone can come to Mormon Row and experience a spring morning or a summer thunderstorm at the altar of the Tetons.

Appendix I
Genealogies

Moulton

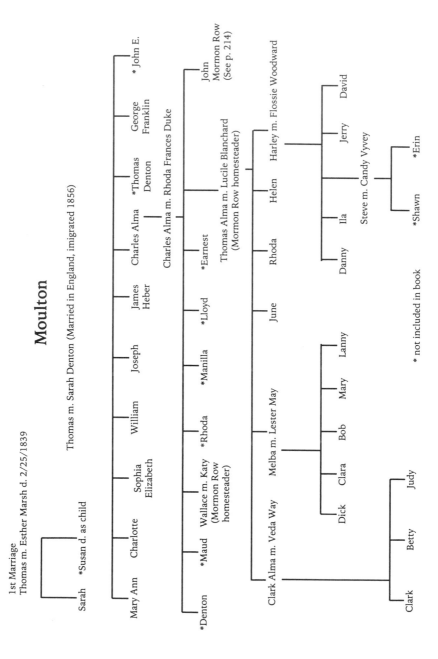

John
Mormon Row
(See p. 214)

* not included in book

May

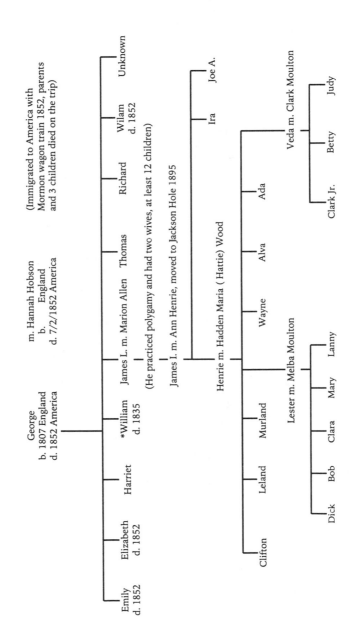

George
b. 1807 England
d. 1852 America

m. Hannah Hobson
b. England
d. 7/2/1852 America

(Immigrated to America with
Mormon wagon train 1852, parents
and 3 children died on the trip)

Emily
d. 1852

Elizabeth
d. 1852

Harriet

*William
d. 1835

James L. m. Marion Allen   Thomas

Richard

Wilam
d. 1852

Unknown

(He practiced polygamy and had two wives, at least 12 children)

James I. m. Ann Henrie, moved to Jackson Hole 1895

Ira   Joe A.

Henrie m. Hadden Maria (Hattie) Wood

Clifton

Leland

Murland

Mary

Lester m. Melba Moulton

Wayne

Alva

Ada

Veda m. Clark Moulton

Dick   Bob   Clara   Lanny

Clark Jr.   Betty   Judy

* not included in book

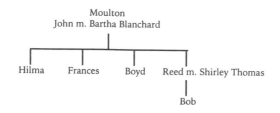

Moulton
John m. Bartha Blanchard

Hilma   Frances   Boyd   Reed m. Shirley Thomas

Bob

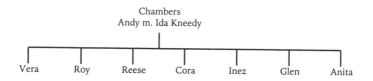

Chambers
Andy m. Ida Kneedy

Vera   Roy   Reese   Cora   Inez   Glen   Anita

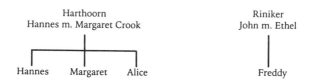

Harthoorn
Hannes m. Margaret Crook

Hannes   Margaret   Alice

Riniker
John m. Ethel

Freddy

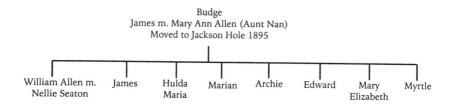

Budge
James m. Mary Ann Allen (Aunt Nan)
Moved to Jackson Hole 1895

William Allen m.   James   Hulda   Marian   Archie   Edward   Mary   Myrtle
Nellie Seaton   Maria   Elizabeth

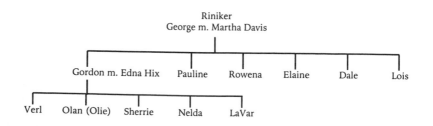

Riniker
George m. Martha Davis

Gordon m. Edna Hix   Pauline   Rowena   Elaine   Dale   Lois

Verl   Olan (Olie)   Sherrie   Nelda   LaVar

End Notes

PART I: FEATHERS AND FUR

Information for this book came from a variety of sources, primarily located at the Teton County Historical Center (TCHC); American Heritage Center/University of Wyoming (AHC/UW); and Wyoming State Archives and Historical Department.

General collections and documents used included the biography and vertical files of those three facilities, the wonderful trunk-full of information accumulated by Elizabeth Hayden and held by the TCHC; the files of the *Jackson's Hole Courier*, Jackson Hole *News*, and Jackson Hole *Guide*; the Merrill Mattes, Thompson, Teton National Forest, and F. M. Fryxell collections at AHC/UW; and several books about Jackson Hole including *Origins, A Guide to the Place Names of Grand Teton National Park and the Surrounding Area*, by

Cynthia Nielsen with original research by Elizabeth Wied Hayden (Jackson: Grand Teton Natural History Association, 1988); *From Trapper to Tourist* by Elizabeth Wied Hayden (Jackson: Grand Teton Natural History Association, 1992); and *Along the Ramparts of the Tetons, The Saga of Jackson Hole Wyoming* by Robert B. Betts (Niwot, CO: University Press of Colorado, 1978).

NATIVE AMERICANS

For the detail about the Indians in Jackson Hole, much useful information was found in the Merrill J. Mattes collection at the AHC/UW. Mattes, a National Park Service Historian, provided detail about the early tribes to visit Jackson Hole. Other articles used were "Teton County Has Colorful Past" Jackson Hole *Guide*, February 25, 1965. Information about the Sheepeaters is from: "The Sheepeaters of Yellowstone Park" by John Bonar, *Wyoming Rural Electric News*, October 1977; "Food for the Sheepeaters," by T. W. "Bill" Daniels, *Wyoming Wildlife*, September 1957; "Mysterious Sheep-Eaters were first Native U. S. 'Hippies,'" publication unknown, copy in TCHC vertical file.

LOOKING FOR PELTS

The voluminous records in the Mattes collection provided detail about the fur trade era. Those files cited information from such other sources as a report on the Jones expedition by Captain William A. Jones; "Yellowstone National Park" by H. M. Chittenden; "American Fur Trade" by H. M. Chittenden; an article by S. N. Leek in the *Jackson's Hole Courier*, April 19, 1934; *Story of the Trappers* by A. C. Laut; and an untitled manuscript by Grace Raymond Hebard, used for the dedication of Grand Teton National Park. Particularly useful was "Jackson Hole, Crossroads of the Western Fur Trade, 1807-1829," by Mattes, reprinted from the *Pacific Northwest Quarterly*, April 1946. The Elizabeth Hayden Collection at the TCHC is replete with information about the fur trade era including references from published sources including the *Jackson's Hole Courier*, the memoirs of Bryant B. Brooks, and a copy of a diary by Thomas Moran. The Hayden collection had a very detailed chronology of early settlement in Jackson Hole beginning with the fur trade era of 1807 and continuing through 1919. Hayden also revealed valuable information about David Jackson, William Sublette, Jedediah Smith, and other early mountain men as well as the fur trader's rendezvous, where they were held, who was in attendance and comments about the activities. Other sources included "Annals of Jackson Hole" by J. R. Jones, *Jackson's Hole Courier*, June 15, 1933; *History of Wyoming*, by T. A. Larson, (Lincoln: University of Nebraska Press, 1965) and *Give Your Heart to the Hawks*, by Winfred Blevins (New York: Avon, 1973).

A NAME FOR THE AREA

See fur trade references above, also the Hayden Collection and *Origins, A Guide to the Place Names of Grand Teton National Park and the Surrounding Area* by Cynthia Nielsen and Elizabeth Hayden.

PART II: A PLACE TO CALL HOME

Detail about the Wilson family move to Jackson Hole is from "Sylvester Wilson" by Melvina Wilson Robertson, *Jackson's Hole Courier*, Aug. 14, 1949; and information provided by Olan Riniker in an interview with the author in

July 1993. General Wilson town information is also from a manuscript "Wilson" prepared by the Teton County Planning Office, Aug. 9, 1991.

PART III: MORMON ROW

A SYMBOL FOR AMERICA
References for this section included oral interviews and correspondence with Clark and Veda May Moulton in May 1981 and the period May 1991-September 1993; and with Lester and Melba Moulton May from May 1991 to September 1993; and the files of the Teton County Historical Center (TCHC). The specific works used for this introductory chapter are cited in more detail in the chapters which follow.

PUSHING WEST FOR FREE LAND
The Mormon Trek West by Joseph E. Brown, (Garden City, NY: Doubleday & Co., Inc., 1980), and *Handcarts to Zion: The Story of a Unique Western Migration, 1856-1860* by Leroy and Ann Hafen (Glendale, CA: Arthur H. Clark Company, 1960) were used for information about the Mormon migration; an autobiographical sketch of the life of James May provided by Veda May Moulton gave detail about the May family migration from England to Utah in 1852. Other references used were *Women's Diaries of the Westward Journey* by Lillian Schlissel, (New York: Schocken Books Inc., 1982); the quotation from Jim Beckwourth is from the guidebook for the Wyoming Centennial wagon train, 1990; Information for the section on homesteading was obtained in a class on Carbon County, Wyoming, history taught by Nancy Anderson, Rawlins, Wyoming, in 1989; from *Colliers Encyclopedia* (New York: MacMillan Education Company, 1986); "Salute to the Century of Homesteading" by Edith M. Thompson, in the Casper *Tribune-Herald and Star*, March 11, 1962; "Honyockers of Harlem Scissorbills of Zurich" by Mabel Lux in the *Montana Magazine of Western History*, Autumn 1963; Various clippings from the American Heritage Center/University of Wyoming, (AHC/UW) Laramie, vertical file H753; and *History of Wyoming* by T. A. Larson (Lincoln: 2nd edition, revised, University of Nebraska, 1990).

WEST WITH A HANDCART
Information for this chapter chronicling the Mormon handcart companies is from *Handcarts to Zion* and *The Mormon Trek West*, cited above; and Moulton family documents including the Thomas Moulton history which covers Moulton family history from 1781 until 1934, compiled by Verda Hicken and provided by Clark Moulton. In July 1993 the author also traveled that portion of the Oregon-Mormon Trail where the Willie Company became stranded in 1856.

DREAMS AND YELLOW ROSES
For this first chapter about the emigration of Mormon settlers into Jackson Hole and the Grovont area, information was obtained in oral interviews the author conducted with Clark and Veda Moulton and Lester and Melba May and from correspondence with those same people from the period of January 1991 until June of 1993. Also used were an oral interview with Henrie May conducted February 11, 1966, by the TCHC staff, a transcript of which was located at the Wyoming State Archives in Cheyenne.

Excerpts from the diary of Maggie McBride are from the *Jackson's Hole Courier*, July 27, 1950. Additional information came from interviews with Lester May and Clark Moulton conducted by JoAnne Byrd in 1983. Transcripts of those interviews were provided by the interviewees; however, they are also located at the Teton County Library and the TCHC. Information also was provided in an unpublished manuscript written by Lester May about early life and the people who settled on Mormon Row, and in interviews with Mabel James of Pinedale, Wyoming, conducted by the author on September 29, 1991 and May 21, 1993.

A POOR MAN'S LEGACY

This chapter was written using information provided by the Moulton family including Clark and Veda Moulton, Harley and Flossie Moulton, Lester and Melba May, Helen Wise, and June Moulton. Specific references included the interview JoAnne Byrd conducted with Clark Moulton, referred to in Chapter 6 references; "T.A. Moulton" by Melba May, Jackson Hole *Guide*, August 25, 1966; "Teton County Has Interesting Past," by Melba May, Jackson Hole *Guide*, August 25, 1965; an unpublished manuscript provided by the family, "History of Thomas Alma and Lucile Blanchard Moulton;" "Former Mormon Row Rancher, T.A. Moulton, Laid to Rest," Jackson Hole *Guide*, November 17, 1966; an unpublished manuscript, "History of My Life" by Elizabeth Fife (mother of Lucile Blanchard Moulton); unpublished manuscript, "A short history of Charles and Rhoda Moulton" by Maud Christensen; "Mormon Row," an interview with Clark Moulton by Bill Willcox in *Jackson Hole, The Magazine of the Tetons*, 1991; "Mormon Row Holdouts" by Bill Willcox, Jackson Hole *News*, June 14, 1989; "The ranching life, a visit with Clark A. Moulton" by Joan Lawson, Jackson Hole *Guide*, June 19, 1980; "Threshing grain—it took from September to Halloween," Jackson Hole *News*, August 30, 1973. Additional detail came from Lester May's unpublished manuscript, cited above and information about the water rights for T.A. Moulton was provided by the Wyoming State Engineer's office, Cheyenne, Wyoming, Gordon W. "Jeff" Fassett, State Engineer.

A MELTING POT

Sources for this chapter included the unpublished manuscript of Lester May, cited above; an interview with Viola and Jim Budge conducted by Jo Anne Byrd, October 1982, copies at TCHC and Teton County Library. Various notes on the Budge family located in the Elizabeth Hayden collection at the TCHC including copies of newspaper clippings, a listing of descendants from the family book of Mary Ann (Aunt Nan) Allen Budge; an article, "Allen Budge's Life," Jackson Hole *News*, March 13, 1975; "Homesteading the Valley with the Budges" by Fern Nelson, Jackson Hole *Guide*, July 4, 1974; "Mary Ann Budge" *Jackson's Hole Courier*, April 19, 1951; "Aunt Nan: Even the Fish Ate Out of Her Hand," by Fern Nelson, October 3, 1974, Jackson Hole *Guide*. Additional information about the Budge family came from by Mabel James of Pinedale, Wyoming. Other detail came from an interview with Roy Andrew H. Chambers by Jo Anne Byrd, February 8, 1988; "Biography of Andy Chambers," Jackson Hole *Guide*, December 8, 1966; and "Longtime resident Ida Chambers dead at 90," publication unknown, clipping at TCHC. Also used were "Jim Chambers writes about early telephones," March 24, 1955; a series of articles about early settlers which ran in the Jackson Hole *Guide* in 1965; and the Kent Album of early settlers' statements about their arrival in Jackson Hole, located at the TCHC. Olan Riniker provided biographical information about his family in unpublished manuscripts related to Martha Davis Riniker, George Riniker, and John Riniker. Other detail came from the biography files of the TCHC, AHC/UW, and the Wyoming State Archives. Information about Joe Pfeiffer came from *The American West*, Winter, 1964, Vol I, No. 1; *The American West*, Fall, 1965, Vol. II, No. 4, and biography files at the TCHC.

THE MOUNTAIN SLID

Information about the Gros Ventre slide came from a manuscript by William O. Owen located in box 12 of the Merrill Mattes collection at the AHC/UW, UW, Laramie, Wyoming; newspaper articles including "Gigantic landslide dams Gros Ventre river three miles above Kelly Tuesday," *Jackson's Hole Courier*, June 25, 1925; "Riding the Range" by Floy Tonkin, Jackson Hole *Guide*, date unknown, clipping from TCHC; "Fifty Years Later the Scar Still Remains," by Fern Nelson, Jackson Hole *Guide*, June 19, 1975; various clippings from the Hebard Collection at the AHC; and an account of the Kelly Flood in the May 18, 1992, Idaho Falls *Post Register*. Particularly helpful was forest ranger C. E. Dibble's account of the Gros Ventre slide and flood provided by the TCHC.

A WALL OF WATER

Many of the sources used for chapter 9 were used for this chapter as well. Additional information came from the files of the TCHC including clippings from the Jackson Hole *Guide* for articles published in 1965 as part of the "Teton County Has Colorful Past. . ." series. Also used was "Gros Ventre River Flood takes Huge Toll in Life and Property," *Jackson's Hole Courier*, May 19, 1927. Some material is from the collection of Elizabeth Hayden at the TCHC, and from the W. O. Owen Collection No. 94, at the AHC/UW, Laramie, Wyoming. Also used were personal papers and documents provided by Veda Moulton, including the original Red Cross tally book kept by her mother after the Kelly flood.

SEASONS OF TIME

Sources used for this chapter are many of those already cited in earlier chapters including the various clippings from the Jackson Hole *Guide, Jackson's Hole Courier,* and Jackson Hole *News;* the Elizabeth Hayden Collection and general files at the TCHC; the unpublished manuscript by Lester May; and interviews with Clark Moulton and Lester May. Also used was a transcript of a talk by Lester and Melba May at the March 16, 1972, meeting of the Teton County Historical Society. During that oral presentation, May recited his poem, "I Bear Bleak Witness," which is published here, for the first time.

PRESERVED FOR AMERICA

Information about the creation of Grand Teton National Park as we know it today is from a variety of sources including a series of articles, "Thunder in the Hole," by Lorraine Bonney, published in the Jackson Hole *News* in 1983; the series, Teton County Has Colorful Past. . ." published in the Jackson Hole *Guide* in 1966; an article, "Harold Fabian, builder of Teton National Park," by Emory Anderson, Jackson Hole *Guide*, October 12, 1972; "For What do we Fight," a publication in May 1943 about the proposed

Jackson Hole National Monument; "State Fights U.S. 'grab' of 216,000 Acres," Tucson *Daily Star,* Tucson, AZ, March 30, 1943; "Friends of Rockefeller Plan Correct Misrepresentations," *The Wyoming Press,* Evanston, Wyoming, Oct. 28, 1931; letters from Horace M. Albright, director of National Park Service, and from Harold P. Fabian, vice-president of the Snake River Land Company, April 6, 1933 to the *Jackson's Hole Courier* Editor, Wilford W. Neilson; and the general files of the TCHC. Also used were the Merrill Mattes, Olas Murie, Teton County, and Thompson Collections at the AHC/UW.

PART IV: ROUGH TIMES

AN OUTLAW HERE AND THERE
Detail for this section is from the Idaho Falls *Post Register, Jackson's Hole Courier,* Jackson Hole *Guide,* Casper *Tribune-Herald and Star,* and Chicago *Herald.* Also used was "Teton Jackson" by R. K. DeArment in *True West,* March 1993, and the general files of the TCHC and AHC/UW.

CUNNINGHAM RANCH
Information is from the TCHC files and a book, *Cunningham Ranch Incident* by Doris B. Platts, (Wilson, WY: 1992) and the files of the *Jackson's Hole Courier,* Jackson Hole *Guide* and Jackson Hole *News.*

DEADMAN'S BAR
Information is from the TCHC; *Teton Magazine,* and the files of the *Jackson's Hole Courier,* Jackson Hole *Guide* and Jackson Hole *News.*

INDIAN HUNTING CONFLICT
Detail about the Race Horse case and Indian uprising of 1895 is from "Chief Race Horse. . .In the contest of the Pale Face Treaties," by Edith M. Thompson, *Wyoming Tribune,* July 21, 1896; "An Indian Fight in Jackson Hole" by Agnes Wright Spring in *Old West,* Spring 1967; and "First Indian War" by Stephen N. Leek, from vertical file at TCHC. Other documents are located at the Wyoming Archives.

PART V: GUIDES AND DUDES

LEIGH AND JENNY LAKES
Detail about Beaver Dick and Jenny Leigh is from the TCHC, AHC/UW and Wyoming Archive biography files. Other useful information was located in the Thompson collection of the AHC/UW, which has Beaver Dick's original diaries. Also used was "A Man Called Beaver Dick" by Robert B. Betts, *Teton, The Magazine of Jackson Hole,* 1977.

OWEN WISTER, AN EARLY DUDE
Detail about Owen Wister is from the files of the TCHC and AHC/UW and from *Owen Wister Out West* by Fanny Kemble Wister. The Mitchell diary related to Wister's hunting trip to Jackson Hole appeared in the Jackson Hole *Guide* in July 1965.

SIGNAL MOUNTAIN

Information about Signal Mountain is from the TCHC. Other sources include *Teton Magazine,* the files of the *Jackson's Hole Courier,* Jackson Hole *Guide* and Jackson Hole *News;* and an unpublished manuscript by John D. Sargent, dated Fall 1892.

BRING ON THE DUDES

Information is from the files of the TCHC and AHC/UW.

PART VI: LOOKING FORWARD

LET THE WOMEN RULE

Information about the all-woman town council is gleaned from clippings in various publications including numerous issues of the *Jackson's Hole Courier,* the Jackson Hole *Guide,* July 1, 1965; Long Beach (California) *Daily Telegram,* June 8, 1920; *The* (New York City) *Evening Mail,* May 14, 1920; and *The Delineator,* September, 1922.

NATIONAL ELK REFUGE

Detail is from the Mattes, Thompson, Teton National Forest, and F. M. Fryxell collections at AHC/UW and the files of the TCHC.

MENOR'S FERRY

Menor's Ferry information comes from TCHC files including "Bill Menor," Jackson Hole *Guide,* March, 1, 1965; "Not Mean, but Menor" by Frances Judge, *Empire Magazine,* Denver *Post,* Dec. 2, 1951; a National Park Service information brochure, "Menor's Ferry Trail" (Moose: Grand Teton Natural History Association, 1983); and souvenir program, "Menor's Ferry Restoration in Grand Teton National Park," from the Mattes Collection, AHC/UW.

CHAPEL OF THE TRANSFIGURATION

Information comes from the Hayden collection, *From Trapper to Tourist,* and from the *Jackson's Hole Courier.*

JACKSON LAKE DAM

Information about the Jackson Lake Dam is from the TCHC files, and articles including "Building of Jackson Dam Brings Colorful Recollection," Idaho Falls *Post-Register,* April 4, 1972; and "Dam Reconstruction" by Nancy Kessler, Jackson Hole *Guide,* July 13, 1988.

Bibliography

Albright, Horace M. Letters located at TCHC.

Allen, Marion V. *Early Jackson Hole*. Redding, CA: Press Room Printing, Inc., 1981.

Betts, Robert B. *Along the Ramparts of the Tetons, The Saga of Jackson Hole Wyoming*. Niwot, CO: University Press of Colorado, 1978.

—-. "A Man Called Beaver Dick," *Teton, The Magazine of Jackson Hole*, 1977.

Blevins, Winfred. *Give Your Heart to the Hawks*. New York: Avon, 1973.

Brown, Joseph E. *The Mormon Trek West*. Garden City, NY: Doubleday & Co., Inc., 1980.

Christensen, Maud. Unpublished manuscript, "A Short History of Charles and Rhoda Moulton."

Colliers Encyclopedia, New York: MacMillan Education Company, 1986.

DeArment, R. K. "Teton Jackson," *True West*, March 1993.

Dibble, C. E. Unpublished account of Gros Ventre Slide and Flood, TCHC.

Fabian, Harold P. Letters and documents located at TCHC.

Fife, Elizabeth. Unpublished manuscript, "History of My Life."

Fryxell, F. M. Collection, American Heritage Center/University of Wyoming.

Grand Teton Natural History Association. "Menor's Ferry Trail." Moose: Grand Teton Natural History Association, 1983.

Hayden, Elizabeth Wied. *From Trapper to Tourist.* Jackson: Grand Teton Natural History Association, 1992.

Hafen, Leroy and Ann. *Handcarts to Zion: The Story of a Unique Western Migration, 1856-1860.* Glendale, CA: Arthur H. Clark Company, 1960.

Hicken, Verda. Unpublished manuscript, Thomas Moulton, family history from 1781 until 1934.

Judge, Frances. "Not Mean, but Menor." *Empire Magazine,* Denver *Post,* Dec. 2, 1951.

Larson, T. A. *History of Wyoming.* Lincoln: 2nd edition, revised, University of Nebraska, 1990.

Mattes, Merrill. Collection, American Heritage Center, University of Wyoming.

_____. "Jackson Hole, Crossroads of the Western Fur Trade, 1807-1829," reprinted from the *Pacific Northwest Quarterly,* April 1946.

May, James. Unpublished manuscript, autobiographical sketch.

May, Lester. Unpublished manuscript about early life and the people who settled on Mormon Row.

Nielsen, Cynthia with research by Elizabeth Wied Hayden. Origins, a guide to the place names of Grand Teton National Park and the Surrounding Area, Jackson: Grand Teton Natural History Association, 1988.

Platts, Doris B. *Cunningham Ranch Incident.* Wilson, WY: 1992.

Riniker, Olan Riniker. Unpublished manuscripts on Martha Davis Riniker, George Riniker, and John Riniker.

Sargent John D. Unpublished manuscript, Fall 1892.

Schlissel, Lillian. *Women's Diaries of the Westward Journey.* New York: Schocken Books Inc., 1982.

Spring, Agnes Wright. "An Indian Fight in Jackson Hole", *Old West,* Spring 1967.

Stone, Elizabeth Arnold. *Uinta County: Its Place in History.* Laramie: The Laramie Printing Company, 1924.

Teton County Planning Office. Unpublished manuscript, "Wilson" August 9, 1991.

Willcox, Bill. "Mormon Row", an interview with Clark Moulton. *Jackson Hole, The Magazine of the Tetons,* 1991; "Mormon Row Holdouts" Jackson Hole *News,* June 14, 1989.

Wilson, Charles Alma and Elijah Nicholas. *The White Indian Boy* and its sequel, *The Return of the White Indian.* Rapid City: Fenske Printing, Inc. 1985.

Wister, Fanny Kemble. *Owen Wister Out West, His Journals and Letters.* Chicago: University of Chicago Press. 1958.

Writers' Program, Works Project Administration, State of Wyoming, American Guide Series. *Wyoming A Guide to its History, Highways, and People.* New York: Oxford University Press, 1941.

Wyoming Recreation Commission. *Wyoming, A Guide to Historic Sites.* Big Horn Book Company, 1976

Oral Interviews:
Clark and Veda May Moulton, by the author, 1981, 1991-1993.
Lester and Melba Moulton May, by the author, 1991-1993.
Mabel James, by the author, September 29, 1991, and May 21, 1993.
Harley and Flossie Moulton, by the author, 1993.
Henrie May, by the TCHC staff, February 11, 1966.
Lester May, by JoAnne Byrd, 1983.
Clark Moulton, by JoAnne Byrd, 1983.
Viola and Jim Budge, by JoAnne Byrd, October 1982.
Roy Andrew H. Chambers, by JoAnne Byrd, February 8, 1988.

Correspondence with the author:
Harley and Flossie Moulton
Lester and Melba May
Helen Wise
June Moulton
Olan Riniker
Clark and Veda Moulton

Newspapers:
Casper *Tribune-Herald* and *Star*
Tucson *Daily Star*
Wyoming Press
Wyoming Tribune
Jackson's Hole Courier
Jackson Hole *Guide*
Jackson Hole *News*
Long Beach (California) *Daily Telegram*
The (New York City) *Evening Mail*
Idaho Falls *Post Register*.

Magazines/Periodicals:
Wyoming Rural Electric News, October 1977
Wyoming Wildlife, September 1957
Montana Magazine of Western History, Autumn 1963
The American West, Winter 1964, and Fall 1965
The Delineator, September 1922

Index

227

About the Author

Candy Vyvey Moulton
Mormon Row, 1993
(Photo Credit: Betty Vyvey)

Candy Vyvey Moulton is a Wyoming native who was reared on her grandparents' homestead near Encampment. She started raking hay on her family's ranch at age six and knows first hand about raising crops, irrigating hay, and moving cows. For the past twenty years she's worked for various Wyoming newspapers as an editor, reporter and photographer.

She writes regularly for the Casper *Star-Tribune*, Rawlins *Daily Times, Wyoming Livestock Roundup,* and the *Fence Post.* She is assistant editor of *The Roundup Magazine,* official publication of the Western Writers of America. Her work has appeared in the Denver *Post*, the *Arizona Daily Star, Tours and Resorts Magazine,* the Chicago *Tribune, Western Horseman, True West, Adventure West, Southwest Art, Vistas West, Fodor's Travel Publications* and *Time* magazine. Moulton is the co-author of *Steamboat: Legendary Bucking Horse* and is currently working on other books about Wyoming and Western history.

Moulton and her husband Steve have two children, Shawn and Erin Marie, a couple of fifth generation Wyoming natives. They make their home near Encampment, Wyoming along with three horses, a cat, and a rabbit.